ANDRÈ THE KINGSLAYER

· AUBREY T. COPELAND ·

A NOVEL

ANDRÉ, THE KINGSLAYER

Published by Owl Writer Press

Find the author online at:

www.theowlwriter24.wordpress.com

www.twitter.com/theOwlWriter

ISBN: 978-0-578-48445-7

Printed in the United States of America

For my mother, who taught me how to read and write.
Without her, this book wouldn't have been possible.

AUTHOR'S NOTE

This is a fantasy book, but it is composed differently than the standard novel of its genre. Unlike many high fantasies, *André, the Kingslayer* is written as a first-person narrative that uses almost a hundred footnotes. While these annotations are mainly a world-building tool, they are also used to describe a historic event, a magical spell, or something else entirely.

I assure you, these footnotes are only meant to help your understanding and nothing more.

—A.T.C., 2019

ANDRÈ THE KINGSLAYER

VENSYR'S PROLOGUE

June 17th, 1427

THE WAR WAS almost over.

After eight long years of endless battles, the king would soon be dead. The reign of Tiberius would be known as the darkest in the history of the Empire. Never before had a king been so hated, and never had such hatred been so deserved. But thanks to a man named André (also called *the Kingslayer*), the Black King Tiberius would soon be a memory.

In the grand scheme of things, my cousin was no longer my concern. The responsibility of killing him now rested with the Kingslayer. There were many reasons I had to leave the resistance, yet the prevailing one was that Tiberius—my own flesh and blood—wanted me dead. And so, I decided to fake my death, just like my wife did eight years ago.

On June 17th, I received a parcel with a letter from her that read:

Dear Vensyr,

This package contains a potion you can use to clone yourself. Since your cousin is determined to see you dead (and a reunion with him is now inevitable), you will be able to use this clone to fake your death like I did when the war began. This means the Emperor will no longer try to kill you, and together we can leave the Empire. Once the copy assumes your identity, make your way to Issylot. You'll know where to find me. Good luck!

Love always,

Jocelyn

I folded the letter on its creases and stuffed it in a pouch beneath my cloak; then, I looked inside the parcel to find a metal flask with the potion inside. I took the item in my hands, opening a silver locket that hung around my neck. Inside was a picture of Jocelyn: a beautiful woman with curly red hair.

I'll see you soon, I thought.

The truth is I would miss the resistance, but that would pale in comparison to how much I'd already missed Jocelyn. So, I cracked open the flask and prepared to drink the potion, but before I did, I smiled.

I was going home.

PART ONE

The Kingslayer Prophecy
April-May 1427

1

Wᴉɴᴅ ʜᴏᴡʟᴇᴅ ᴀs I woke one morning, totally unaware that my life had changed forever. I could hear hushed voices downstairs as I prepared to get up, running my fingers through my brown and gray strands of hair. One voice didn't belong, however. It was the voice of a visitor.

Suddenly, there was a knock at my bedroom door.

"Who is it?" I asked.

"Alex," said a familiar voice.

"Come in," I told her, sitting upright to face the door.

Alex entered my bedroom. A skinny little thing with short blonde hair, she was the daughter of my godfather, Hugo von Salcroth. Because of this (*and* the fact that her father had raised me), Alex was like a sister to me.

"Hey André, someone's here to see you," she said, messing with the strings of her leather corset.

"Really, who?" I asked.

Alex shrugged. "I don't know. Some wizard."

I put on the nearest tunic I could grab and slipped on

a pair of leather brown pants; then, Alex and I followed the staircase just outside our bedrooms, and together we made our way to the other end of the house. We reached a dining room with a long table capable of seating twenty people or more. Once we took our seats, I looked from my aging godfather to his son Luke. I then saw the wizard who wanted to see me.

He was an older gentleman with a pearly-white beard, who sat in a wheelchair and wore elaborate garments from head to toe. He was clearly a feeble old man, but he had once been a powerful wizard. How could he not have been? Based on his clothes (and the dragon signet ring on his middle finger), I could tell he was a Wizard of the Fifth Order.[1] This was the most prestigious Order of Wizards in all the Isobellian territories.[2] Without a doubt, he was the most powerful wizard I had ever met.

"My name is Rubin Mindu," he said, removing his half-moon glasses.

---

1 There are five Orders of Wizards within the Isobellian Empire, each having members with a certain level of training that corresponds with that Order's number. For example, the Wizards of the First Order are the most basic in terms of power and ability; meanwhile, the Wizards of the Fifth Order are the most elite.

2 There are seven Isobellian territories: Cynlon, Cynlu, the Gililands, Hathara, Abu Dali, Yorkenshire, and Lychford. These territories—along with the sovereign state of Isobellia—make up the Isobellian Empire. Since the Imperial Realm is mostly made up of territories, people will occasionally refer to it as the Isobellian territories.

"Andreas Bellbrook," I replied, shaking Mindu's hand from across the table. He pulled a torn envelope with a broken wax seal from his waistcoat. "It's nice to meet you," I added, leaning back in my chair.

Mindu didn't respond. He opened the envelope and took out a folded-up piece of paper.

"What brings you here?" I asked.

"Unfortunately, the war," he said.

What does he mean by that? I wondered. Then again, the Empire *had* been at war for the last eight years. Dominion of Tiberius[3] was absolute in Isobellia. Anytime someone crossed him or his Imperial Knights, that person was charged with treason.[4] Because of such dark times, the child of the Black King's predecessor—Sara Willington—gathered her finest knights and began a revolution.[5] But what did any of it have to do with me? I wasn't even in the resistance.

"I should explain," Mindu said, holding up the piece of paper. "My wife sent me this letter several days ago, which was delivered by one of the resistance's undercover agents.

---

3 Also known as the Black King and the leader of the Imperial Knights.
4 In the days of Tiberius, treason was a charge brought against all of the Black King's enemies. Almost every act against the Empire was considered treason (including fleeing arrest), and everyone found guilty faced the guillotine for their crimes. This is why—during the reign of Tiberius—only the resistance dared to cross the Empire. If anyone else did, they were likely to end up dead.
5 A conflict that would later be known as the Great Revolution.

According to her, the Wizards of the Fifth Order have been all but wiped out."

"*What!?*" Luke said.

"What does that have to do with me?" I asked.

"I'm getting to that," Mindu replied. "Our castle in Drake's Keep was attacked and only two mages survived.[6] One was my wife Ellyn, while the other was Tarja S. Lyra, our leader. This letter contains information about a prophecy. It's just unfortunate that my wife died getting it to me."

"That's terrible," Hugo said.

"Yes, I know," Mindu replied, looking at me. "Archwizard Lyra had several visions while Dragonshorde Castle was under siege. She then told my wife Ellyn everything, and Ellyn relayed that same information to me, just in case I could dig deeper."

"And you think this prophecy is about me?" I asked.

"I do. You see, the prophecy centers around a brave hero. He'll be able to steal the legendary sword Excelsior

---

6 The Sacking of Dragonshorde Castle was a lengthy military campaign directed at the Fifth Order's headquarters in Drake's Keep. The Empire's objective was simple: surround the Fifth Order and wipe them out for aiding the resistance in many key battles during the Great Revolution.

Having lasted from December 1426 to April 1427, it was the longest battle to take place during Isobellia's civil war. It wasn't until Cyrus Isperion betrayed the Fifth Order that General Rothenheim and his knights were able to breach the castle walls. In the end, the Imperial Knights overpowered the Fifth Order, killing every wizard in sight except Archwizard Tarja S. Lyra and her second-in-command, Ellyn Mindu.

from the Imperial City,[7] and will end the war by killing Tiberius. He matches your description: a young man in his mid-twenties, who has a lock of gray hair. That's why I think it's you, André."

Everything Mindu said seemed to fit me perfectly. My hair *did* have strands of gray, plus I'd just turned twenty-four last month. But something didn't feel right. I knew nothing about Mindu, except that he was a Wizard of the Fifth Order. *If* I was going to hear him out, I would need more information. So, I reached my hand out and said, "Let me see the letter."

Mindu did as I asked; then (after unfolding the letter), I drew in a deep breath and read it aloud:

My dearest Rubin,

I'm afraid I have bad news. The Empire's attack on Dragonshorde Castle has ended in success, and hundreds of Wizards of the Fifth Order have been killed. Archwizard Lyra and I have both been arrested, and for all I know, you're the only Fifth Wizard who remains a free man.

But I'm not writing you to discuss the Fifth Order. After all, we still have hope to win the war. For weeks, Lyra has had visions of a Kingslayer,[8] who may be able to

---

7 Originally called Lyonisis, the Imperial City is the capital of the Isobellian Empire. It is an ancient city, and has been at the helm of seven separate Empires since the birth of St. Aramara himself.
8 The word *"Kingslayer"* has two definitions. They are as follows:

overthrow Tiberius. She told me every detail before she was killed in our cell at Alba Gorath,[9] just in case I could pass it along.

The Kingslayer is from a town in the north. He is left-handed, and is in his mid-twenties. This man—a man with a gray lock of hair—and a few others will be able to steal Excelsior from the Imperial City. With the legendary sword, the Kingslayer will have the power to challenge the Black King and end the war by killing him, despite his immortality.

This will be my last goodbye, Rubin. Once the Imperial Knights realize I've told you everything about the Kingslayer, I'm certain they will kill me. Now it is your job to find him. Keep your eyes open for any sign that he is near. All I can do now is pray that St. Aramara's light will shine in you. May the Gods of Redisy bless you, and may the Mother Creator watch over you as you search for this Kingslayer.[10]

---

1.   A person who has killed a king in the past.

2.   A person who is prophesied to kill a king in the future.

9 An island prison where the Empire's most "dangerous" prisoners are kept.

10 There are three classifications of deity according to the teachings of the Church of Redisy.

Anismyra (better known as the Mother Creator) is the creation goddess of the Redisy faith. She created the gods, the universe, and she is the spiritual mother of St. Aramara himself.

Your wife,

Ellyn Mindu

P.S.: Be careful. The Imperial Knights were able to extract this information from Lyra as well. By now, Tiberius will also be looking for him.

I folded the letter on its creases and gave it back to Mindu. Part of me felt he was right. There were, after all, several details that matched facts about me. Even Ellyn's description of my hair was accurate.

But what if Mindu was lying?

"The Kingslayer sounds like me," I said, looking at Mindu. "I can see why you think we're the same person."

"But?" Mindu pressed on.

"I don't know anything about you. I don't even know what led you here, to *me* of all people."

"You were in the newspaper."

This was true. Several weeks earlier, I had been in a national chess tournament. I loved chess, and was pretty

---

The Gods of Redisy (or simply the gods) are a body of hundreds—maybe thousands—of deities, each with their own set of powers and characteristics. They created the Earth (as well as the mortal realm), each placing within it a bit of themselves.

Aramara Tij Luthinium (also known as St. Aramara) was the chief patriarch of the Church of Redisy. Born of a virgin, the Noble Saint was sent to die in the mortal realm to atone for the sins of the world.

Collectively, they are known as the Holy Trinity of the Faith of Redisy.

good at it too. In fact, a fair deal of my time went to playing chess at the local tavern (when I wasn't working there).
And my practice paid off, since I *did* come in first place.
It was my proudest moment, and to make it even better
was the fact that my picture ended up on the front page
of *The Isobellian Times*.[11] But now I wished I hadn't been
in the paper. Clearly, it's what led Mindu to my godfather's doorstep.

"Listen," Mindu said, "I know what I'm asking is treason, but you have to come with me. Tiberius knows about
the Kingslayer, just as I do. Even if you're *not* this hero, the
Emperor is bound to send his knights to kill you."

"How can you be so sure?"

"I'm a lot older than you are, Boy. I've been in the resistance for years, and have even worked alongside Princess
Sara Willington: the *rightful* heir to the Imperial Throne. If
Tiberius thinks you're the Kingslayer (as I do), then he will
send his knights to kill you so they can avert the prophecy."

"Oh really?" I snapped.

"André!" Alex whispered; I ignored her.

"Yes, *really,*" Mindu replied. "Even with there being a
prophecy, it doesn't mean those things will occur. If his men
can kill you (or *whoever* the Kingslayer is), then Tiberius
can keep the prophecy from being fulfilled. That's why I say
he'll send his knights."

---

11 The Empire's largest, most successful daily newspaper.

"Look," I said, "I hate the Empire, especially Tiberius. He killed my parents,[12] which is why I live with Hugo in the first place. I'd like the resistance to win the war, but I just can't go with you. I have a family here who loves me, and I don't want something to happen to them because I joined the resistance."

"André, you shouldn't worry about that," Hugo said, pulling a silver ring from his waistcoat. "This ring allows anyone who is untrained in the magical arts to teleport from place to place. If they come for us, all I have to do is slip it on and we can escape. You know this."

"There are rules to the magic within that ring," I replied.

"Yes, but at least we have a means of escape. If you're *really* concerned something will happen to us, don't worry. We'll be fine."

But Hugo didn't understand. I just wanted to forget Isobellia's civil war. I wanted to live *my* life, the way *I* wanted to. I didn't want to be a hero at all.

"I can't do this," I said, looking at Mindu. "I just can't do as you ask."

Mindu slammed his fist on the table. "This man doesn't deserve to be king and you know it!"

"So what if I do? It doesn't mean I'm the Kingslayer."

"This man is a murderer. You *do* realize that, right? He killed King Michael Willington and his wife in a

---

12 Jorge and Leslie Bellbrook, according to public records.

hostile takeover. Does that not mean anything to you, Mr. Bellbrook? Don't you even care?"

"Of course I care," I said, clenching my fist. "But need I remind you that he killed my parents too? I'm not going to end up the same way."

"Don't be a stubborn fool," Mindu replied. "Tiberius is immortal, with thousands of men and creatures at his disposal.[13] In addition, the resistance is already losing this war. If you *are* the Kingslayer and you turn your back on them, you not only become a coward. You also sentence your people to an eternity of darkness. Do you not see the truth?"

"I think I do, actually," I said, rising from my chair as everyone watched me doing so. "I see the truth that the only answer you'll accept from me is yes. Unfortunately, I can't do that." I turned to face the hallway. "Not while *you're* here, anyway."

"Where are you going?" Alex asked.

"To my bedroom," I told her. "I need time to think."

---

13 During the reign of Tiberius, most of the Black King's army was made up of Imperial Knights; however, the Empire also had many dragons, zombies, and shades at their disposal (plus Dragonshade Wurms like the ones that guarded the Imperial City). They were usually unseen in densely-populated areas, since they were a danger to the human population. Most of them were instead stationed at key military centers such as the fortress of Versailles and the island prison of Alba Gorath.

2

"LUKE AND I are going out for a bit," Hugo said.

I was sitting on my bed, looking at a photo of my mom and dad. It had been a good thirty minutes since I walked out on my conversation with Mindu, yet my blood was still boiling with rage from the nerve of his request.

I looked at Hugo. He was standing in the doorway.

"Where are you going?" I asked, setting the framed picture onto my bedside table.

"Into town," Hugo replied. "Mindu's got a train to catch."

Good riddance, I thought.

"Alex isn't going with you?" I asked my godfather.

He shook his head. "Only Luke is going with."

I had a bad feeling about this. If anyone was going to say something about the day's events, it would've been Alex. It just wasn't in her character to remain silent on something as important as a prophecy. And sure enough, when Hugo and Luke had left with Mindu, Alex came into my room and confronted me about what had happened.

It wasn't a pleasant conversation; that's for sure.

I tried telling her that I needed time to think, that I couldn't join the resistance *just cuz Mindu told me to*. But as usual, Alex von Salcroth refused to listen.

Why couldn't she just accept that I didn't want to hear it? If she really loved me, she would've given me time to think. But as the conversation went on, I realized she would do everything in her power to make me accept my destiny: even if it meant the death of me.

I saw that look in her eyes: Alex meant business.

From that moment on, she was obsessed with Lyra's prophecy. For weeks, it was always *Lyra's prophecy this* and *Rubin and Ellyn Mindu that*. Things eventually got so out of hand that I began spending less time at home (staying out late after work), and before I knew it, I was spending all my free time going to mass.

No problem there, of course. I *loved* going to the cathedral, passing through its long arched doorways and sitting within its granite walls. There was a time many years ago, when watching the Members of Redisy[14] worship the gods would intrigue me. Seeing them in that same holy praise lately made me happy. *Happy*, because it helped me forget the harassment I had to endure at home. When I was there,

---

14 Churchgoers, or simply followers of the Redisy faith.

the priests on staff provided religious counsel, which gave me the kind of attention I so desperately needed.

But that was before May 2nd arrived. That was the day Alex entered the church with a bishop by her side.

"André!" she called to me; I turned to see her.

The bishop was dressed in elaborate robes of white and red.[15] He and Alex walked past the pews of the church, resting at the front where I sat behind one of the church's two stone basins.[16] I looked at the pair of them, standing in front of me; then, I rose from my seat, brushing back my brown and gray strands of hair.

That's when I said, "Alex, I—"

"What are you doing here?" Alex interrupted.

I rolled my eyes. "Seeking religious counsel."

"Come on, André," Alex said, looking at Bishop Edricson. "I'm not a fool. You've been avoiding me and Dad."

"So *what!?*" I spat.

"I demand to know why! Even Edricson here can tell you're avoiding something. Why don't you just come home with me and we'll discuss this like *mature* adults? Dad is even willing to—"

"Not to be rude, but I'm done talking," I said.

"But Andr—"

---

15 Formal attire that all clergymen wear.
16 Water-filled bowls used in various rituals.

"No, Alex," I interrupted. "You've done your talking. Now I need a break from the family."

"You're being stubborn."

"No I'm not. *You* are. Remember, I never said I *wouldn't* do as Mindu asked. I just need time."

"Time? *Time* is a luxury we do not have, *Andreas!*"

Alex was angry. I was certain of this because she never called me *"Andreas"* unless she was mad at me. But I was ready for her. I'd been preparing for this moment for weeks, after all. "Oh, you going to go off on me now?" I said. "Spare me your bullcrap!"

"Sir! *Please* don't talk like that!" Edricson told me. "This is a place of worship," he added.

"I am aware of this," I said, pointing at Alex with one finger. "But *she* is so determined to see me as a hero that she has brought our family feud into the holiest place in the grand cathedral!"

"André…" Alex said quietly.

I began shedding tears. "All I want… all I *need* is time, Alex! I've been coming here to get away from *you!* I've avoided coming home because you are so determined to see me as something that I may not even be. I need to be left alone, yet you cornering me here, hounding me like you have is making it impossible for me to do the thinking that I need to do!"

I let out an outburst of anger, kicking the side of a

nearby pew so hard that I almost splashed water out of the closest stone basin. Soon, I stormed out of the auditorium, glaring at Alex while I did; then, I left the church altogether.

***

Alex slipped a note under my door that read:

I'm sorry.

But despite how sorry she was, I felt like she deserved every bit of what she got. She'd been hounding me for weeks, so me feeling sorry for her wasn't going to happen. *It served her right.* I was in a world where Alex had gotten her just reward. Now maybe... *just maybe* I could have some time to think.

I locked my bedroom door so I could do just that. For part of the evening, I could hear Alex crying. But I didn't care, nor was I going to. If Alex was going to learn how to treat people, she had to endure the pain.

"I'm sorry," she repeated the following day.

I looked at her. Her short blonde hair was a royal mess. After all, she'd spent half the day in her room, thinking about how she'd acted. It was clear to me now that Alex had learned her lesson.

That's why I decided to forgive her.

Together, we walked outside, into the cobblestone streets of Willowbrook. The town was smaller than most others: just one reason Hugo had his house built there. Nearly every home in Willowbrook was simpler than his, belonging to local farmers and the like. But having been a lord on Michael Willington's Royal Council,[17] it only made sense that my godfather would have the nicest home in town.

That day, I couldn't see a single Imperial Knight, not even in the alleyways. This was unusual, since you normally couldn't walk two blocks without seeing at least one of them. Of course, that's not to say I was complaining that they were gone. Alex and I decided to take advantage of this opportunity, slipping onto the roof of the local tavern. Once we both sat on the clay-shingled rooftop, Alex moved her leather satchel onto her lap.

"Will you at least think about what Mindu said?" she asked.

That was all I'd wanted for weeks. "I have been," I replied. "You know that."

Alex pulled an envelope from her satchel containing the same wax seal as the letter from Ellyn Mindu. "Mindu wrote me. This here's the letter," Alex said.

"You've kept tabs?"

"Yeah." Alex pulled the new letter out of its envelope.

---

17 A body of lords appointed by the king and voted into office by the people. Their main purpose is to pass laws that are then signed or vetoed by the king. The Royal Council did not exist during King Tiberius's reign.

"It's not about you," she added. "He just wanted to tell me that Sara Willington's been arrested."[18]

"*What!?*" I said at once.

"I know," Alex replied, letting out a loud huff. "This is proof that the war is getting worse. I'm not sure what the resistance will do when Tiberius has her killed."

"How long have you known about this?"

"Since yesterday. I tried telling you, but you wouldn't talk to me. This is the first real conversation we've had all week."

"Yeah, but can you blame me?"

"Not anymore. Still, Isobellia needs you."

"I know."

That was the first time I'd admitted it out loud.

"If you know it to be true, then join the resistance and become the Kingslayer," Alex said. "Isobellia needs you

---

18 Between March and May of 1427, Princess Sara Willington was on the run from the Empire following her role in the Battle of Versailles. During the conflict, Her Majesty succeeded in her mission to assassinate Lord Barron (one of Tiberius's chief advisors during the war), which is believed by historians to have been devastating to the Black King in his hopes of maintaining control over the Empire.

In response to this crushing defeat, Tiberius signed an arrest warrant, but Sara wasn't easy to catch. It wasn't until May 1st that her days on the run came to an end. While in the city of Windull, General Darius and his knights cornered the princess, stripped her of her weapons, and took her into Imperial custody; then, they began moving her to the Imperial City to face public execution.

desperately, and you heard what Dad said. If they come after us, he can use his magic ring and teleport us elsewhere."

"I know," I replied. "But that ring is no guarantee that you, Hugo, and Luke will be safe. To use it, you'll need enough energy, and you must be in range of where you want to go. You know this as well as I do."

"I do. I'm just afraid Tiberius is going to kill you like he did your mom and dad."

"Is *that* why you wouldn't drop it?" I asked.

"That's part of it," Alex admitted. "The way I see it, if you *are* the Kingslayer, the entire resistance will be watching your back. Getting out of Willowbrook *really* seems to be your best option if you want to survive this war."

It was in talking to Alex that I realized something. Her goal was never to make me accept my destiny. Instead, it was to get me out of Willowbrook (for my own safety), because the Black King Tiberius wanted me dead. I stood up on the rooftop and Alex joined me in doing so. I embraced her as she kissed my left cheek. I could tell by her trembling embrace that she was terrified of the days to come. Not that I could blame her. I was frightened too.

I looked at Willowbrook's skyline and spotted the copper-brown dome of the grand cathedral, towering high above all other buildings. "If I *do* join the resistance," I said, "there will be much bloodshed."

"Then blood will be shed," Alex replied. "Things will

certainly get worse if you *do* decide to join, but there are also benefits to the carnage that is to come. Churchgoers will pray to their gods, and maybe that will help you out in the long run. But André, regardless of what *does* happen, you need to be prepared for the worst."

"Hey Alex?"

"Yes?"

"Do you *really* think Tiberius will send his knights, like Mindu said?"

"I'm not sure," Alex replied. "I guess it's possible. But as you know, I haven't been involved in the war, so my knowledge on the Emperor's dealings is small. However, one thing I'm certain about is that Lyra's prophecy described you very well. If Mindu was lying for whatever reason, you'd have to admit he's a very clever old man."

"Why do you say that?" I asked.

"Because finding someone *else* with this hero's description is like finding a needle in a haystack. It *won't* happen again, at least not with someone who's left-handed like you are." Alex turned around and looked at the sky, facing the direction opposite me. "If the letter *was* a trick," she said finally, "Mindu's as clever as they come."

3

THE WALLS OF Hugo's house shook on their foundations. I looked around for a moment, wondering what had woken me; then, I saw a bright light, coming into my room through the nearby window.

What is going on? I wondered, slipping out of bed.

I looked out the window and saw dark, masked figures[19] outside. They were illuminated by a large fire, covering the north end of Willowbrook.

Panic rushed through my mind. The town I'd lived in since childhood was being torn apart! The farmers' crops were on fire; the church was set ablaze; and when I felt the house shake again, I realized the figures outside were the Imperial Knights that Mindu had warned me about.

I have to wake the family, I thought. If I didn't, they could be killed with what was going on. But before I got

---

19 During the Great Revolution, many Imperial Knights wore various masks to conceal their faces. The practice was started for assassinations and illegal arrests, to hide proof of Imperial involvement.

the chance, Hugo entered the room, armed with a flintlock pistol. This was pretty good timing, given the situation. Now, only Luke and Alex needed waking.

I grabbed a magic wand[20] from my bedside table.

"Mindu was right," Hugo said, looking out the window. "It's Tiberius's men. They must've come for you to avert the prophecy."

I slipped a clean robe over my body. "Why are they attacking the town?" I asked. Hugo and I stepped out of my bedroom and into the hallway.

Hugo didn't answer my question. Then again, he *was* pressed for time. If I was to have guessed, the Imperial Knights didn't want any witnesses if I *was* killed. Mother Creator knows the kinds of problems it would cause if I was made into a martyr.

Hugo entered Luke's room as I went into Alex's. For a moment, I just looked at her sleeping. Soon, however, I began shaking her shoulder, and only a moment later she came around. *"Alex,"* I whispered, *"you need to get up."*

"Wh—*why?*" she complained. "It's too early...."

"Imperial Knights are attacking the town," I told her.

"What!?" she said at once. Alex got out of bed, though I could tell she didn't want to. Once she was wearing a robe

---

20 A long stick (made of wood or ivory) that is used to cast magic spells. Although they can be used to enhance the magical abilities of wizards, it is also common for non-wizards to use them. That way, those untrained in wizardry can cast spells.

over her body, she looked right at me. "I told you so, I *frea-kin'* told you so! Even the Imperial Knights believe it!"

"Alex—"

"Now's not the time to argue!" Hugo pointed out, peeking into the room. Luke was barely awake. "We have to get out of here—"

CRASH! There was a sound of breaking glass and wood downstairs. The Imperial Knights were inside the house! Trying to remain calm, Hugo handed Alex and Luke a pistol and a wand respectively. That way, they could protect themselves as we escaped the house and looked for a place to teleport from.

Hugo pulled a lever on his flintlock pistol, activating a spring-loaded bayonet[21] at the end of its barrel. He led me, Alex, and Luke down the spiraling staircase and toward the arched doorway of the house's main entrance. The front door was kicked in, with splinters and shattered glass scattered across the floor. Standing in the doorway were Imperial Knights, armed to assassinate. They were all wearing black cloaks,[22] with carnival masks concealing their

---

21 A device held in a backward position on a flintlock's barrel by a spring-load mechanism. In the heat of battle, the user may pull on its lever to engage the bayonet, turning the pistol into a close-range weapon. It was originally designed in 1419 by Aldric Rookwood, ex-inventor and later a general in the resistance. The weapon proved useful in the Great Revolution, giving the knights of the resistance a combative edge over the Empire.

22 Typical uniform that every Imperial Knight wore during the Great

faces. Most of them carried a wand, but their obvious leader did not. Instead, he carried a flintlock pistol, with three barrels that were locked and loaded. He removed his mask with a swift motion, and that's when I recognized him.

Magnus Morfang.

He was third-in-command of the Imperial Army,[23] and had jet-black hair that was wild and untamed. He wore a red scar over one of his eyes, which told me that he was *very* experienced in the art of war. Seeing his face presented me with a royal wakeup call. Tiberius wouldn't have sent one of his inner-circle if he didn't see me as a serious threat. Just being considered a Kingslayer was treason enough for Tiberius.

"Surrender, Bellbrook," Magnus said.

I fired a red stream of light at him, knocking him into his men.[24] Several knights swore as they scrambled to their feet. Magnus was livid, so I ran down the adjacent hallway as Hugo, Alex, and Luke followed.

"Hurry!" Hugo told us.

"You're going to *bloody* pay for that, you fool!" Magnus yelled, firing bullets into the air as we left through the backdoor.

We ran as fast as we could, but Imperial Knights came

Revolution.

23 According to historic records, General Morfang was only out-ranked by General Ravana Valassaari and King Tiberius himself.

24 *Strikklys:* A basic spell that knocks over its target.

at us from every direction. They fired spells at us, as well as bullets. As we passed the local tavern, I could hear an incantation and knew at once that an even more powerful attack was coming. A red beam of light flew overhead, crackling as it went; then, as it hit the ground, the spell exploded with the mighty force of a bomb.[25]

The blast sent me flying through the air, and for a moment, I lost sight of Hugo, Alex, and Luke. Hot air hit me as I landed on the flat of my back. Soon, I noticed Luke lying right beside me.

Where are Alex and Hugo? I wondered.

Yes, I could *hear* Alex screaming in horror as the enemy tore Willowbrook apart, but I still didn't know where they were.

Luke and I scrambled to our feet.

"We need to move," I told him.

"Okay," he replied, "but where should we—?"

Suddenly, two bullets came flying through the air and hit Luke right in the chest.

"Luke!" I screamed, catching him as he fell. He was covered in blood, soaking into the fabrics of his nightgown. I shook him, trying to get him up, but this was futile. He was weak. He was dying. But I wasn't giving up.

---

25 *Explochéo:* A fire sorcery that explodes on impact with its target. It is a powerful spell, usually known exclusively by Wizards of the Fourth Order or higher.

I aimed my wand at Luke and shot a puff of white smoke into the bullet holes, but this Healing Spell didn't do enough to heal him fully.[26] He was still dying, still fading into darkness. I now understood why Mindu had tried to recruit me. The Empire was responsible for killing hundreds, maybe thousands of Isobellians. My parents were just two of their victims. Now, it looked like Luke would soon be joining them.

"Come on, Luke, don't leave me!" I yelled, just as a couple tears fell from my eyes. But my words were meaningless, because Luke was dead. I didn't want to accept this reality, but I had no choice. *"Luke…"* I repeated, although it was pointless. "Just… wake up…."

A group of Imperial Knights now approached, including the man who shot Luke. He was quite an ugly man, with a bionic arm carrying a flintlock pistol.

"Surrender," said General Gertrude, cocking his gun and aiming at me.

"You killed my brother!" I yelled, raising my wand at him.

He seemed not to hear me. "We are servants of the Black King, now drop your weapon and no harm will come to you."

"I've done nothing wrong!"

---

26 *Curis:* A sorcery capable of mending wounds and removing scars. It is difficult to use if you're a non-wizard.

"Of course you haven't. At least, not yet."

"You can't arrest me when I've done nothing!"

"That's bull and you know it!" Gertrude said. "The Imperial Knights will do as they please, *and* kill all they like. Take your brother for example. Tiberius doesn't care about him *or* your stupid so-called rights. All he cares about is power, and crushing all who oppose him!"

I didn't know what they would do to me, but I wasn't willing to find out. With my wand already aimed at Gertrude, I fired the first spell that came to mind. It was a destructive spell—a red ball of fire—that hit him in the face and scorched him from the inside out.[27] His men screamed and cussed at me as I fled into a patch of trees. I took cover (hiding behind a fallen tree trunk), when I heard hushed voices off in the distance.

"Come out, you *bastard!*" called one Imperial Knight. It was only a matter of time before they found me, so without delay, I took off running as bullets and spells came at me from behind.

A jet of blue light knocked me off my feet.[28] For a moment, the world was spinning out of control. I tried getting up, but I had no strength to do so. And to make

---

27 *Deathfyre:* A spell capable of killing anyone who touches its searing hot flame. While very powerful, this sorcery is easily learned by non-wizards, but only by those who've carefully studied how to use it.

28 *Incapitus:* A spell capable of removing all energy from its target. It is an effective tool when the user is making arrests.

matters worse, the Imperial Knights were fast approaching. One then stood right over me.

I had expected him to kill me, but suddenly, a bullet flew through the air and hit him right in the chest. Initially, I thought it was friendly fire, but I soon realized that I was wrong. A group of soldiers came through the trees, all of them heavily armed. They wore different cloaks than the Imperial Knights, each with a red phoenix[29] on their left shoulder. It was in seeing this Royal Crest that I knew I was saved. I was aided by the resistance.

"Who the devil are you!?" said an Imperial Knight.

"You know who we are," said one soldier in the darkness of the trees. "We were just passing through, but you've attacked a helpless town. That doesn't sit well with me!"

I could only watch helplessly as the two sides engaged each other. At first, it seemed like they were evenly matched (dagger-to-dagger, sword-to-sword), but it soon became clear that the resistance were better skilled than the Imperial Knights. One enemy combatant was cussing like hell's fury as a resistance soldier pulled me up, taking me behind a tree for cover. We sat there for some time, listening to enemy soldiers screaming as they were torn apart. As everything

---

29 The Royal Crest of the House of Willington. In 1422 (three years into the Great Revolution), the resistance adopted the symbol as their Coat of Arms. It was rumored that Sara Willington chose this banner to represent the rebirth of her family's dynasty, as her family would return to power if the resistance won the war.

grew calm, the group of resistance fighters came to see if I was all right.

A man with dirty-blonde hair came closest to me, illuminating his face with a light from the tip of his wand.[30] "I am Vensyr D'Artanian,"[31] he said, looking me in the eyes. "We are watching over you now."

---

30 *Illuminatus:* A basic spell that can light up a small area. It gives a wand the same function as a torch lit with fire.

31 The resistance's highest-ranking general, second only to Sara Willington herself.

                                   4

ALL NIGHT, I could hear the people of Willowbrook
screaming as they were murdered by Imperial Knights.
Every echo of their screams reminded me of Luke, and how
I was unable to save him. Vensyr seemed to be a good man,
leading his knights to intervene; meanwhile, I remained
behind so I could get my mind off what was happening.
Earlier, Vensyr had asked if I could help his men, but he
could tell the answer was no. That's why he left me behind
with two of his knights. He knew the night's events had put
me through a living hell.

    At daybreak, Vensyr returned to the woods with Alex
and Hugo. As planned, they had used Hugo's magic ring
to avoid the Imperial Knights, but I could tell by looking
at Alex that she knew all had *not* gone according to plan.
She knew Luke was dead. Come to find out, she'd even seen
his body. Together with Vensyr and his men, Alex and I
buried Luke.

"I'm going to miss you, Little Brother," Alex said. Right then, I saw a single tear trickling down her cheek.

"I'm sorry for your loss," Vensyr told us, messing with a silver locket that hung around his neck.

Despite his words, however, I didn't get to feeling any better. Luke was dead, and there was nothing Vensyr could do to bring him back to life. A few minutes later, Hugo told Vensyr that our home had been destroyed (and we were therefore homeless). For this reason, Vensyr suggested we join his men.

Funny, isn't it?

Joining the resistance meant committing high treason, and not wanting to do so was part of the reason I refused Mindu a few weeks earlier.

"I was kind of hoping to avoid that," I told Vensyr.

"It's too late for that," he insisted. "You've already committed treason simply by fighting off Imperial Knights. If you go off on your own, it could get you killed. Besides, you've already killed James Gertrude. If Tiberius discovers this, you'll be drawn and quartered in front of every citizen of the Imperial City."

He was right, of course: a fact I hated more than anything.

"Why were you here last night?" Hugo asked Vensyr.

"Sara Willington was arrested several days ago," Vensyr replied. "My men and I have received word from our scouts that the Imperial Knights are taking her to the Imperial City for public execution."

"I heard about that," Hugo said.

"We were on our way to rescue her. That's when we found André. By this point, they should be near the Evergreen Forest.[32] That's where they plan to hand her over to Ravana Valassaari."[33]

"That's two weeks' walk from here," I said.

"Not if we go by train. The next town is Port Galvis. That's five miles, yes?"

"It is."

"We'll board a train and head for Issylot. That's the forest's closest city, I think."

"There is one problem though," Hugo said.

"And that is?" Vensyr replied.

"André and Alex aren't soldiers. If you want their help rescuing the princess, they're likely to end up dead."

Vensyr seemed mindful of this possibility. "They'll just have to wing it," he said. "That's how I learned to fight."

Hugo looked irritated, but said nothing.

"Say we succeed and rescue the princess," I said. "What then?"

---

32 A massive forest that spans half the territories of the Empire (from the Gililands in the north to Cynlon and Cynlu in the east and south). Even the sovereign state of Isobellia is covered in part by the Evergreen Forest, as both Issylot and the Imperial City are near its evergreen trees.

33 Tiberius's highest-ranking general and leader of his inner-circle.

"Ever heard of Marik Katsa?" Vensyr asked.

"Isn't he the sky pirate that captains *The White Gauntlet*?" Alex replied.

"The very same. He's an old friend of Sara's, and has offered to meet us in Issylot and take Her Majesty to Alma Defa."

Suddenly, one of Vensyr's men came up to us, riding on horseback. "We've found several horses in one of the surviving stables. It belonged to one of the dead."

Vensyr smiled. "Gather what supplies you can."

"There's not enough time. Several enemy soldiers are headed this way. From the look of things, they're after someone or some*thing* important."

"They are," I told Vensyr. "They're after me."

"What do you mean?" Vensyr asked, looking puzzled.

"Archwizard Lyra had several visions about André," Alex said. "Apparently, he's the Kingslayer: a prophesied hero capable of overthrowing Tiberius."

"André's the Kingslayer? That would explain why they're headed this way." Vensyr looked at the man on horseback. "Where are the other horses you found?" he asked him.

The man on horseback pointed at seven or eight resistance knights, tying several horses to some trees.

"Put as many men on horseback as you can," Vensyr continued. "If the Imperial Knights are indeed after the Kingslayer, we must protect him at all costs. But for now, we should board a train in the next town. Saving the princess is our priority at the moment."

***

An hour later, we arrived in Port Galvis. Clearly, Vensyr knew how to avoid an enemy. We arrived at the coastal city unscathed, with not a single Imperial Knight in sight along the way. But despite our luck evading them, Vensyr was determined to keep them off our trail. Not long after we arrived, he led us into the shadows of an alleyway; then, after jumping off his horse, Vensyr took out his pistol and cocked its hammer.

"Stay here," he said, returning the gun to its holster. "I have an errand to run. I'll be back in ten minutes."

When he returned, Vensyr was holding several train tickets tightly in his hand.

"Here, take these," he said, passing them to everyone in our party. He then threw a cloak over my shoulders and lifted the hood. "You'd better hide your face," he told me. "We can't have the Empire catching you, least of all now."

Hugo, Alex, and I followed Vensyr and his men out of the alleyway. They led us down a side street (past the city's docks), and before I knew it, we had arrived at the local train station. Once inside, we boarded the fastest train to Issylot, sitting down in a compartment where we could talk freely.

Thank the gods I made it, I thought, looking out the window behind me. *I'll be safe till Issylot for sure.*

Unfortunately, this wasn't true. Just outside the locomotive were several Imperial Knights, standing not far from the engineer. One of them was Magnus Morfang, who led the attack on Willowbrook the night before. The moment I saw his face, I wanted to kill him. After all, he was partially to blame for Luke's untimely death.

But I didn't do anything to him.

I just sat on the train, burying my face into the hood of my cloak. Seeing Magnus again made me feel uncomfortable, but how had the enemy tracked us this far? Like I said, there wasn't a single Imperial Knight in sight along the way to Port Galvis. Could they have seen us leaving Willowbrook and I'd simply not noticed?

"André, you okay?" Alex asked suddenly.

I darted my eyes back at the window, motioning toward Magnus and his men.

"What do you think we should do?" Alex asked, looking at Vensyr.

"Don't worry. We'll be fine," he replied. "If they come onboard, I'll know what to do. Trust me, André's in good hands."

The locomotive started to move. Soon, the train had left Port Galvis and was bound for the industrial city of Issylot. I looked out the nearby window as we passed through the rolling hills of the Gililands. It was funny to think how my life was changing. A week earlier, if you had said I would accept my destiny, become the Kingslayer, and join the resistance, it was likely I wouldn't have believed you. But here I was, now a member of that same revolution. Yes, Tiberius would try and have me killed, but at least now I was around people I could trust.

Two hours into our trip, the locomotive screeched to a halt. I rose from my seat, stepping out of the compartment as others began doing the same. Magnus was coming down the corridor, followed by several Imperial Knights.

"What is the meaning of this!?" one passenger yelled, just down the corridor.

"This is Imperial business," Magnus said, pointing his flintlock pistol at the man who'd spoken. "Mind your own!" I threw myself back into the compartment, leaving the sliding door ajar. After a moment, Magnus spoke again, saying, "We are looking for Mr. Andreas Bellbrook. One of his companions was seen boarding this train. Has anyone seen him?"

Magnus was showing everyone a picture of me, taken from Hugo's house.

I started to panic. What was I going to do? If I was caught, chances were good that I'd see Luke again sooner than I thought.

Vensyr closed the compartment door, kneeling down

and looking me dead in the eyes. *"Don't make a sound,"* he whispered.

He took out his wand, casting some kind of spell upon the door and windows in our compartment.[34] It seemed like nothing happened at first, but when Magnus and his men looked through the windows of the sliding door without trying to enter, I knew the spell must have done something.

"What did you do?" I asked. Vensyr helped me off the floor.

"I enchanted the windows," he replied. "That way, the Imperial Knights out in the hallway would think the room was vacant."

"You made us invisible?" Alex asked, running her fingers through her short blonde hair.

"Sort of. To those outside the compartment, it would certainly look that way."

I returned to my seat. I was still a bit shaken up, but was otherwise all right. "How far are we from Issylot and the Evergreen Forest?" I asked.

The train started moving again. Two compartments over, I saw Magnus and his men, mounting themselves on

---

34 *Invisicus Totalum:* An illusion-type enchantment that can make a person or object invisible. When cast upon the window(s) of a room, this spell can fool those on the outside to think the room in question is vacant. In common vernacular, this enchantment is known as a Cloaking Spell.

broomsticks.[35] They opened a nearby window; then, they flew out the window in question.

"Two more hours and we're there," Vensyr said once they were gone. "With any luck, we'll have our girl back by day's end."

---

35 Brooms that are enchanted to let those mounted on them fly as easily as a bird or dragon.

5

I LOOKED OUT the window and saw a city coming into view.

Issylot: The Industrial City.

I opened the compartment door as we drew closer. I couldn't stay on the train long, since I was a wanted fugitive. But Vensyr had anticipated this. The moment we arrived in Issylot, he began ushering everyone in our party off the train; then, we left the station altogether.

We moved into the streets of Issylot, then into the nearest alleyway. The city was unlike anything I'd ever seen before. Airships flooded the sky, and skyscrapers (hundreds of them) were present as far as the eye could see. Needless to say, the city was stunning. Except for the back alleys of Issylot's underworld,[36] that is.

---

36 Or rather, its *criminal* underworld. The alleyways of Issylot are run by all kinds of crime syndicates (most of them tied to Kreelo, the goblin mob boss); however (during the Great Revolution), the Empire tended to overlook the happenings in the slums of major cities. This is why resistance bases were usually found near the hideouts of local crime lords.

Vensyr led us to the nearest resistance base, located behind a local brothel. Once inside, I met several high-ranking members of Sara Willington's resistance. Aldric Rookwood was easily the most battered general of the group, with scars all over his face and two fingers missing from his left hand.

After Vensyr spoke with Rookwood (and another general, Arkham Gibbs), it became clear that the operation to save Sara Willington was about to begin. Members of their brigade armed me, Alex, and Hugo with weapons to save the princess with, and Rookwood saw to it that I received the finest battle garments that money could buy. By the time I was armed and ready, everyone else was ready for action.

"Everyone, listen up," Rookwood said, motioning toward Gibbs.

"We're splitting up into groups," said Arkham Gibbs, running one hand through his salt-and-peppered, thinning hair. He raised his ivory wand and added, "If anyone spots the Imperial Knights escorting the princess through the forest, use your wand and fire a red flare into the sky. That way, everyone else can locate you."

We pulled straws from a mug to decide who went with who. Luckily, Alex and I ended up in the same group. As we parted, Hugo handed me his ring. "Take this," he said. "Might just save your life."

Alex and I left the base with several others, watching our

backs as we went; meanwhile, I kept one hand on the sword that Rookwood gave me, just in case the enemy found us. It wasn't long before we left Issylot's Business District, out of the city and into the trees of the Evergreen Forest. A few minutes after reaching the forest, one member of our party noticed a set of single file footprints, leading off the main road. We followed their trail for hours, with nothing but rabbits to greet us on our journey. But as three p.m. arrived, I heard several voices that had to be close by.

"Did you hear that?" I asked in a whisper.

Alex nodded; so did the others.

We climbed a nearby hill. On the other side, there were several squads of Imperial Knights, met by none other than Tiberius's top general: Ravana Valassaari. She was a tall, lanky thing with long arms and pitch-black hair. I could tell by looking at her that this wasn't a woman to cross. If anyone *did*, they were likely to end up dead.

"Where's the princess?" Ravana demanded. Suddenly, a man I recognized as General Darius stepped forward, leading a girl toward his commanding officer. She was bound at the wrists, and her face was covered by a sack of some kind. "The Black King will be most pleased, Darius." Ravana handed him what looked like a sack of gold. "Enjoy your spoils."

"Thank you, Mistress. I—"

"You have another mission now, Darius. You would do well not to get distracted. Remember Lyra's prophecy?"

I looked at Alex, taking out her wand. She rolled onto her back; then, she aimed her wand into the sky, shooting off a red flare like Gibbs had ordered.[37] For a moment, the Imperial Knights looked around, trying to figure out where the blast had come from. With any luck, our allies would arrive before we were discovered.

Soon, Ravana decided to ignore the recent disruption and return to the Imperial City with her valuable hostage. But before she got the chance, I began seeing members of the resistance appearing just over the hilltop in front of me. Vensyr and Gibbs came into view, riding on horseback; then, Hugo and Rookwood appeared (also on horses), and all four of them led the resistance troops in the fight to save Her Majesty.

"Hand over the princess!" Rookwood said, pointing his sword at Ravana. "You know this is treason!"

"That's a load of *freakin'* bull and you know it!" she replied, pulling a pistol from her cloak. "Tiberius rules this land, not Princess Sara!"

Things were about to get ugly. Even a mere conversation over politics offended the Imperial Knights to the point of

---

37 *Flarkyss:* A fire-based signaling spell, designed to inform others of its caster's location. This sorcery is generally harmless, unless it is cast by a fully-trained Fifth Wizard.

murder. They began drawing swords and loaded guns from their cloaks, when all of a sudden, one of them shot and killed one of Vensyr's men.

"Return fire! *Return fire!*" Vensyr yelled as his men obeyed. Soon, bullets flew in every direction as Alex and I entered the fight.

"André, Alex, get the princess out of here!" Rookwood screamed, throwing himself off his horse and pinning Ravana to the ground.

Alex took out her pistol and shot a couple Imperial Knights; meanwhile, I drew the sword that Rookwood gave me, cutting the bonds around Sara's wrists and removing the sack that covered her face.

Alex, Sara, and I took off running.

"Get the *bloody* princess!" Ravana yelled, kicking Rookwood off of her as she grabbed her flintlock pistol. "And seize the boy who's with her! The Black King's after him too!"

She fired two rounds in our direction, but missed as we jumped behind a fallen tree for cover. It wasn't long before several Imperial Knights began to approach in accordance with Ravana's command. Alex swung her wand in a circular motion, conjuring some kind of shield to protect us from the slew of oncoming soldiers.[38] When it was safe to do so, I brushed Sara off and looked her in the eyes.

---

38 *Shyldig Totalum:* An entry-level enchantment that serves as a protective

"Thank you," she said, straightening her long, brown hair.

"Take this," I told her, handing her a four-barreled flintlock pistol that Rookwood had given me.

Suddenly, Vensyr appeared behind the protection of Alex's shield, riding on a white stallion. "André," he said, jumping off the horse's back, "use this horse to take Sara off the battlefield. When no one can see you both, use Hugo's ring and teleport back to Issylot."

"Will I be able to?" I asked.

"I don't see why not," Vensyr replied. "Anywhere within a five mile radius should be in range of a ring like that."

"In the meantime, what will *I* do?" Alex asked.

"Help me fight," he said, helping me and Sara onto the horse's back. "We'll stall for time. André?" Vensyr added.

"Yes?" I replied.

"Take these," he said, handing me a leather pouch. Inside was a key, a mask made of linen, and a white cloak that was clearly meant for Sara.

I took out the mask and said, "What's this for?"

"That's for Sara; it's enchanted," Vensyr replied. "It allows the wearer to change their appearance at will."[39]

---

barrier from any oncoming attack, magical or otherwise. While very easily cast (even by a non-wizard), this spell is very useful on the battlefield because it can prevent enemy soldiers from bypassing its magical wall.

39 Primarily their face and features adjacent to it like their hair, neck,

Sounds simple enough, I thought, returning the mask to its leather pouch.

"Once you reach Issylot," Vensyr continued, "make sure Sara puts it on. That way, the Empire won't know it's her. Head to *The Black Raven Inn.* That key is to room *307.* Don't do anything else. Just stay there until I arrive. Are we clear?"

I nodded, stowing the pouch beneath my cloak.

"Then good luck, and may the gods be with you."

At once, I snapped the horse's reins, taking off with the princess in front of me. It wasn't easy (leaving Alex and Hugo behind), but knowing I had a mission to fulfill kept me going strong. Suddenly, I heard gunfire flying overhead. That's when I saw General Darius behind us, riding on his broomstick as some of his men did so as well. With every inch I moved, the enemy drew closer. Sara fired a single round at Darius from the pistol I gave her, but she missed. Soon, a fork in the road appeared. One way led to Issylot, the other toward the National Train Station.[40]

I decided to bluff, leading Darius and his men toward the train station. They followed me and Sara through twist and turn, past every tree and measly little twig. Now, it

---

and ears; after all, it *is* only a mask.

40 A train station that connects every major city within the Isobellian Empire. The National Train Station was established in 1372 by Issylot's local business tycoon, Bartholomew H. S. Shadowcrest, not long after the birth of Michael Willington.

seemed like we were outrunning the enemy. I smiled at my success. I would succeed in my mission for sure.

Sara fired her pistol again, this time hitting Darius right below the shoulder. The man fell off his broom, landing on the flat of his back. Immediately, his men stopped to help him. When they were out of sight, I pulled on the horse's reins. The beast then stopped as Sara and I jumped off its back.

"Take my wrist," I told Sara.

She obeyed as I slipped on Hugo's ring. Next thing I knew, we were standing in an alleyway in Issylot, right in front of the local church.

I pulled the mask from the pouch that Vensyr had given me. "Let's go," I said, handing it to Sara. "We need to find the inn."

6

SARA PULLED THE mask over her face, and suddenly, the fabrics within it began to twist and change. Soon, she was like a commoner, with hazel eyes and fiery-red hair. I draped the cloak that Vensyr provided around her neck to hide where the mask met her skin. Then together (with Sara's face altered and mine concealed by the hood of my own cloak), we passed down one street corner and entered *The Black Raven Inn.*

There were several resistance soldiers inside, secretly on guard for Sara's protection. Obviously, Vensyr had taken her rescue seriously. The innkeeper—who was clearly on our side—had the resistance's phoenix crest branded to his skin. He pointed us upstairs, so I led Sara up the staircase and unlocked the door to room *307.*

As we stepped into the room, Sara removed the mask that covered her face.

Finally, after everything that had happened to both of us, we had time to relax. This was good because Sara was a total mess. She was covered in dirt from head to toe: proof of the abuse she'd endured at the hands of General Darius. There were also cuts and bruises here and there, plus dried blood all over these wounds. Because of this, I wasn't at all surprised when Sara expressed the need to bathe herself.

When she had finished, Sara was dressed in a black, frilled shirt and a leather corset. Without a doubt, Vensyr had made sure some of her belongings had been left for her. Her hair was up in a ponytail, and now that I'd seen her all cleaned up, I could finally appreciate how beautiful she was. She was *stunning*, with brown eyes and flowing brown hair that made her the most gorgeous woman I'd ever met. Just the way her eyes dazzled in the candle-lit room made my heart melt, but she was also beautiful on the inside, as I soon figured out.

After all, Sara was very easy to talk to. So (as we waited on our allies to return from battle), Sara and I decided to pass our time by getting to know each other. She told me all about her religious faith: how she joined the churchgoers at the age of twelve, and how she had the Mark of Redisy[41] branded to her wrist at the age of seventeen.

I had never met such a devout servant of the gods and the Mother Creator. Compared to Sara, I was nothing more

---

41 A holy symbol (λ), branded to the skin of every Member of Redisy once they become seventeen. It is the insignia of the gods and the Mother Creator.

than a nonbeliever. Lately, I'd only met with the bishops in church when I needed their guidance. Yes, I was a Member of Redisy, but my faith paled in comparison to Sara's. This line of thinking made me wonder if I was okay in my relationship with my creator. It also made me think of the Imperial Knights and all their wicked deeds.

Was *I* any better?

"No one's perfect," Sara assured me, and this was generous of her. Never before had I met someone so kind. Now I understood why everyone wanted her as their queen. She was radically different than King Tiberius. He was nothing but an evil man, surrounded by his cohorts. But *everything* about Sara was amazing, and every bit of her (in my view) was perfect.

At midnight, Vensyr entered the room with Hugo, Alex, and Rookwood. I could tell by looking at them that the battle had not been easy. Alex looked worn out, and Hugo—in his advanced age—was at risk of passing out if he didn't get some rest soon. But the battle had been a success, and at least my family didn't become another Luke. As I thought about this, Alex hugged me and said, "Thank the gods you're safe."

"Who's this, your girlfriend?" Sara asked, looking at Alex.

"Maybe in incest land," Alex replied with a roll of the eyes. "André's like my brother," she added; then, she looked at me. "General Valassaari took out dozens of soldiers. It made me wonder if you'd make it back alive."

"I'm fine," I told her, looking at Sara. "We both are."

But to be honest, I felt Alex's pain. Not knowing if Alex and Hugo would survive made *me* feel on edge, and frankly, the fact that Ravana Valassaari took part in the battle made my anxiety worse. But Alex and Hugo returned unharmed, just like my newest friends.

"André, Alex," Rookwood said, removing his triangle hat, "I need you to escort Princess Sara to Alma Defa."

With everything that had happened, I forgot that Sara would soon be leaving for Alma Defa. This was an island that was famous throughout the Empire, known primarily as the resistance's sky-bound, elfish base that floated several miles over the Isobellian Ocean. I had never been to Alma Defa, so naturally, I looked forward to accompanying the princess there. But that's not to say I wasn't nervous too. After all, I wasn't sure what would be required of me.

"Once you arrive," Vensyr said, "Rubin Mindu will meet with you, André. Princess?" he added.

"Yes?" Sara replied.

"André here is the Kingslayer, the one Mindu told us about before you were captured."

"He is?"

"Yes. I need you to assist him in any way possible to gain the sword Excelsior from the Imperial City. Once you arrive on Alma Defa, Mindu will meet with you, André, and Ms. Salcroth. It will be up to the four of you to plan this mission. After all, the rest of the resistance leadership has its hands full at the moment."

I looked at Hugo. "Does that include you?" I asked.

"Of course," he said simply. "I *was* on the Royal Council, after all."[42]

I couldn't say I was surprised. Still, that's not to say I was expecting this turn of events.

"We don't have much time to talk," Rookwood said to Vensyr and Hugo.

"I agree," Vensyr replied. "We need to move the princess and the Kingslayer as soon as possible." He turned to face me. "I'll escort you to Issylot's docking bay. Once you figure out how you're going to steal Excelsior, contact me and I'll send you aid."

***

Soon after Vensyr's comment, he escorted me, Alex, and Sara to Issylot's local docking bay. There, I saw the most prestigious airships I'd ever laid eyes on. They were colossal in size (capable of carrying five hundred people per ship), and all of them had an engine run by both steam and manual labor. Each airship had a hot air balloon strapped to it that kept the ship afloat. I looked at Sara to see if she knew which

---

42 Lords on the Royal Council tend to have experience on the battlefield, because most of them are either wizards or ex-soldiers.

ship was Marik Katsa's, and after a moment, she pointed at a brilliantly white airship with a Coat of Arms bearing a gauntlet on the side of its hot air balloon.

It was a beautiful ship called *The White Gauntlet.* As I stepped onboard with Alex and Sara, I felt the warm hospitality of Marik's crew. They were easily more loyal to the resistance than most Isobellians. Most of them—like the innkeeper of *The Black Raven Inn*—had the resistance's crest branded to their skin. Part of me was afraid of them, but luckily they were on my side. The funny thing is, their captain was different than them.

Different to a tee.

He was quite the feminine man, calling me *"Lover Boy"* and *"Sweet-cheeks"* every chance he got. I could've sworn he was attracted to males, but when I met his lovely wife Eelra, I knew this couldn't be true. Some might've said she was merely a cover for his "closeted" way of life, but I didn't think so. Not with the way they were all over each other below deck.

According to Sara (who'd known the sky pirate for years), that's just *"Good ol' Marik for you,"* which was probably true. She went on to explain her thoughts on his queer personality, telling me it was just for show. And this made sense. Marik went as far as to say that he was *"Fine. As. HELL!"* which seemed so ridiculous to me that the only rational conclusion was that Sara was right. Marik *was* putting on a show, and a bad one to say the least.

He carried on like this for the better part of the ship ride, and honestly, I found it entertaining. Most of the time, Marik's feminine persona had me laughing beyond my control, so it should come as no surprise that when we arrived on Alma Defa, I'd barely even noticed.

"Your Majesty," Marik said to Sara, then turning to me. *"Lover Boy,"* he added jokingly, "we have arrived."

I looked out from the main deck and saw an air-bound island coming into view, illuminated by an early morning's twilight. It was surrounded on all sides by a body of water, as if the elfish city was sitting right in the middle of a basin in the sky. Once *The White Gauntlet* had landed in the city's docking bay, Marik and his crew led us into the streets of Alma Defa.

The elves were just outside, waiting on us to arrive.

They were really short creatures (no taller than a child), and just about all of them had flowing blonde hair and eyes like the sea. Most of them wore clothes of either red or green, and almost everywhere I saw an elf, there was a wizard standing right next to them.[43]

Upon saying our goodbyes to Marik and his crew, I looked around and saw the city's finely-crafted, ivory

---

43 Wizards tend to live in elfish settlements.

buildings. I could feel it now. I was in high society, with Sara Willington by my side.

The elves and wizards of Alma Defa were very kind to me, Alex, and Sara, most likely because Mindu was expecting us. But of all the things I had to do, meeting Mindu again wasn't one I was looking forward to. At our last meeting, I'd made a fool of myself. It was at times like this that made me wish I wasn't the Kingslayer, but I couldn't go down that road again. Not after what had happened to Luke, plus everything else that'd happened lately. Mother Creator knows Alex would make sure a repeat of my last conversation with Mindu didn't happen.

The elves and wizards led me, Alex, and Sara toward the resistance headquarters: the revolution's national base where the war began. With a red onion top and a tiny white steeple, the building sat behind a large wall surrounded by a moat. It had once been a courthouse for the Empire, but after the war's first battle,[44] that all had changed.

---

44 Soon after his rise to power, the Black King Tiberius signed a decree so the Empire could arrest and convict anyone he deemed a threat to his reign. Among this number was Vensyr D'Artanian and his wife Jocelyn, who were forced to run from the Empire for thirteen years because of this decree; then, in 1416, their life on the run led to a fateful encounter with none other than Princess Sara Willington.

Together, they began an underground resistance movement, and in June of 1419, the resistance attacked Alma Defa in an attempt to seize control of the elfish island. During the conflict, Jocelyn D'Artanian—a fully-trained, Fifth Wizard—and Ravana Valassaari engaged each other in a

As the elves and wizards led us up the base's marble doorstep, I saw Mindu, waiting in front of the building's long arched doorway. Still in a wheelchair, he was just as feeble as he was at our last meeting. But this time, we exchanged no harsh words, and instead greeted each other like old friends.

"André," he said finally, "I'm glad you have come."

---

magical duel. General Valassaari was clearly ill-prepared. But before she could be incinerated by Jocelyn's powerful, magical flame, Ravana fired her pistol at Jocelyn and allegedly killed her. This tragic blow led the resistance to fight the Imperial Knights with everything they had, and in the end, the Imperials were forced to flee.

In the aftermath of the Battle of Alma Defa, Vensyr D'Artanian was seen burying his fallen wife; however, this was merely a ploy so that Jocelyn could survive the war. In reality, she had taken a potion the night before and created a clone of herself, foreseeing her death in the coming battle. Once the clone had assumed her identity, Jocelyn made her way home to Issylot to live with her brother.

VENSYR'S INTERLUDE

March 5th, 1427

A cool breeze came in through the nearby, opened window as I woke one morning. The night before had not been easy on Jocelyn. Once again, the Empire had tried to kill me. Luckily, I found my way back to Issylot to be with my wife, but it was only a matter of time before the Empire succeeded in its goal.

That's why I agreed to fake my death like Jocelyn did. If I didn't, I was as good as dead.

"So, Vensyr, when'll I have yah back for good?" Jocelyn asked. Her curly red hair was a royal mess, but my wife didn't seem to care.

"Let me tie off a few loose ends and I'll come find you. I have to make sure we win the war."

Jocelyn passed me a locket from her bedside table. "I want you to have this," she said. "For good luck."

I smiled at Jocelyn, leaning in and kissing her lips. The war had been difficult on our marriage, but at least we had that night together. Head to top of my chest, twirling her fingers through my dirty-blonde strands of hair…. It was moments like this that made me wish there wasn't a war. But if we were going to defeat the Empire, I had to see this through.

PART TWO

The Quest of High Treason
May-July 1427

7

MINDU WHEELED HIMSELF through the marble-floored hallway of the resistance base, and after a moment, Alex, Sara, and I followed him into what looked like a meeting room. Lining every wall were many suits of armor, and in the middle of the room, there was a long table with maps—*and* reports from the scouts—laying on top of it. Within these granite walls, I was safer than I would be anywhere else. This wasn't just where many of the resistance's important decisions were made. It was also the place where Sara began the Great Revolution.

Mindu rolled himself up to the nearby table. "I'm really glad you're safe," he told me. "When I heard the news of Willowbrook, I feared you might be dead."

Alex, Sara, and I sat down next to Mindu. Judging by the look of him, Mindu was nervous. He must've prayed for hours, hoping I was all right. Not that I could blame him. Isobellia was in *my* hands, after all. If I had been killed, the resistance would've lost the war for sure. But I was safe now on Alma Defa, so why was he still nervous?

"Are you all right?" I asked, just to get the conversation moving.

Mindu shook his head. "The Empire's made several attacks like the one on Willowbrook. A few resistance bases—*and* the towns supporting them—have been hit by Imperial Knights, and their leaders have been killed for committing high treason."[45]

Sara slammed her fist down on the table in anger.

"Why are they doing this?" I asked.

"Isn't it obvious?" Mindu replied. "It was a diversion. They were trying to keep the resistance from sending you aid."

Alex laughed. "I guess they didn't count on Vensyr showing up then, huh?"

"Apparently not. Still, there's more to this string of attacks than meets the eye."

"Why do you say that?" Sara asked.

"Because not every attack coincides with the one in

---

45 This string of attacks (later known as the Purge of Resistance) came in several waves, spanning from May to August of 1427. Excluding the first wave (which centered around the attack on Willowbrook), the Empire had two objectives in the Purge of Resistance. One was to destroy key resistance bases; the other was to pressure the resistance into handing over Andreas Bellbrook (A.K.A., the Kingslayer).

Willowbrook," Mindu said. "Some of them started after, with one goal in mind."

"He's looking for me?" I asked.

Mindu nodded, handing me a rolled-up piece of paper. "This was brought to me this morning. It was found outside our base in Tipp City."

I unrolled the piece of paper (stamped with a lion crest);[46] then, I read the note aloud:

Hand over the Kingslayer, or more attacks will come.

Sara rolled her eyes. "Why would Tiberius think we'd do that?" she asked.

"Does it matter?" Mindu replied. "The resistance isn't going to hand over someone that could win them the war."

"Speaking of, how are we going to gain Excelsior?" I asked.

"That's *the* question, isn't it?" Mindu said. "Unfortunately, it's going to be a bit more complicated than just breaking into the palace and getting out with the sword unseen."

"Why is that?" Alex asked.

"Because our best bet is going to be stealing the sword at night, while the palace sleeps. And I warn you, the task

---

46 The Empire's Royal Crest, adopted in 1403 after Tiberius's rise to power.

will not be easy. There will be a dozen Royal Guards, watching over the armory where the sword is kept at all times. Tiberius always has the key to that armory, even while he sleeps. That means that it's likely you'll wake him during the heist. Needless to say, we're going to need time and patience if we're going to pull this thing off without fail."

"*Time* is a luxury we do not have," Alex said.

"True," Mindu agreed. "People are dying because the Empire is obsessed with forcing André out of hiding, but we're not entirely without hope. I may have an idea as to how you should handle breaking into the Imperial City."

"And that is?" Sara asked.

I pulled Hugo's ring out of my left pocket. "You mean this?"

"Exactly," Mindu said.

"But with the ring, couldn't we just teleport into the armory?" Sara asked. "That would help us avoid the risk of dying, right?"

"If only it were that simple. I've received word that several Wizards of the Fifth Order have betrayed the resistance.[47] They, under orders from Tiberius, have placed enchantments over the armory, thus keeping you from teleporting inside."

Mindu's words seemed to bother Sara.

---

47 Cyrus Isperion, among others.

"Don't worry," he assured her. "Vensyr has already promised his help."

"I thought he had his hands full at the moment," I said.

"The resistance leadership is capable of running things while Vensyr is gone."

"Okay, but how have you contacted him so fast?"

Mindu held up a leather-bound journal, and immediately I recognized it as a Bynch Book. This was a magical item (enchanted on every page), and with it, Mindu had the ability to send messages back and forth with resistance generals like Vensyr and Rookwood.

"A Bynch Book is *always* the fastest method," he said.

"And you're certain there's no *other* way of ending the war?" I asked. "Besides gaining Excelsior, that is?"

"I'm afraid not," Mindu said. "Tiberius is immortal, so there's no other option. If it wasn't for that magical ring he wears at all times, my guess is we'd have killed him years ago."

"What ring?"

"The Immortality Ring," Sara replied. "It's one of the Relics of Redisy,[48] just like Excelsior."

---

48 There are seven Relics of Redisy (holy items of the Redisy faith) that were once scattered across the Isobellian Empire: Excelsior (the Sword of St. Aramara), the Wand of Power, the Immortality Ring, the Golden Spyglass, the Pendent of St. Aramara, the Sands of Time, and the Everlasting Flame. Each Relic was made by the Mother Creator and bears its own unique power/ability. The Immortality Ring, for example, grants the person wearing it everlasting life; in addition, it can protect their

"Sara's right," Mindu said, and I could tell I had his full attention. "Wasn't it your parents who died trying to keep the ring from Tiberius while you were a baby?"[49]

"How did you know about that?" I asked.

"Hugo told me," he replied. "At our first meeting, you said that Tiberius killed your parents. So, I asked your godfather about it, and he told me everything. And if you don't mind me saying, the circumstances *are* rather interesting. After all, who better to kill the Black King than the son of those he's slain?"

"True," Alex agreed, combing her fingers through her short blonde hair.

---

body from any kind of physical injury. This is why only Excelsior can harm the one who wears the ring. The legendary blade can cut through any solid object, including the flesh of immortals like Tiberius.

49 In 1403, the man later known as Tiberius—*and* his faithful followers—began gathering the Relics of Redisy so they could seize the Imperial Realm from its sitting Emperor, King Michael Willington. Foreseeing his Empire's impending doom, Willington dissolved the Royal Council for the protection of its members; then, he sent one of his most trusted Royal Guards into hiding with the Immortality Ring (which was an heirloom of the House of Willington).

Jorge Bellbrook—the Royal Guard in question—and his wife Leslie settled in Tipp City, where Leslie gave birth to their son André. Unfortunately, their joy was short-lived. Tiberius, now having assumed the Imperial Throne, had several of Jorge Bellbrook's fellow guards tortured until one divulged their location. When he arrived at their home in Tipp City, the newly-crowned Black King killed Mr. and Mrs. Bellbrook (leaving their son to fend for himself); then, he took the Immortality Ring, making himself immortal.

"Well anyway," I said finally, "is that everything?"

"Not quite," Mindu said. "I'll have Vensyr and Gibbs come here in a few weeks to help us plan the mission properly. In the meantime, I'd like the three of you to get to know each other. The ties of friendship are what will get you through this war."

"Until then, where will we go?" I asked.

"*The Red Dragon Inn* has made sleeping arrangements for you. It's been hours since any of you have slept, yes?"

"It has," I said, and at once the idea of sleep became more wonderful than anything I'd ever experienced. *A pillow….* It was like a lover from many years ago, one that I'd longed for since our last encounter. My eyelids were heavy, my body was tired. So naturally, all I could do in response to Mindu was take him up on his offer. "All right," I said, looking at Alex and Sara, "let's go to the inn."

8

"Hey Cutie, *wake up!*"

I opened my eyes, one day in late July. I was laying in my bed at the inn on Alma Defa. The smell of the sea was overly apparent that morning (coming from the water outside), but not as apparent as the smell of dandelions coming from Sara's long, brown hair. She was leaning over me as the sun shined through the nearby window. The princess was quite the flirt that morning. Not that I could complain. She was very beautiful, after all.

"Sara…" I began; then, I fell silent. After clearing out my eyes, I sat upright and looked at the princess. "What is it?" I asked. "And how did you get into my room?"

Sara ignored my second question, bopping me with a nearby pillow. "It's time for you to get up!" she said, spreading her legs and sitting on mine. "Vensyr and Gibbs have arrived."

"They're here to discuss the mission to the Imperial City?"

"Duh," she replied, rolling her eyes. "You know, André, sometimes I feel like you're a little dense." She kissed me on the cheek. "But you still rock my world!" she added. I didn't know what to make of this comment. Was I to be complimented or insulted? I just shrugged it off, seeing how it didn't matter. "You know I love you, right?" she asked.

"What do you want?" I said at once.

"Nothing," she replied, standing up off the bed and bopping me with the pillow again. "Except for you to get up. Mindu expects us at headquarters in fifteen minutes." She handed me a stack of clothes from the wardrobe next to my bed. She then walked to my bedroom door. "I'll let you get dressed," she said finally.

Then she was gone.

***

As Sara and I entered the meeting hall at headquarters, there was an entire slew of people present, including Vensyr, Gibbs, Alex, and Mindu. It was clear that morning that Vensyr and Gibbs had spent many days and nights on the battlefield. On his face, Vensyr wore a couple new scars, while Gibbs's lucky bowler had a new cut right across the brim.

"You're late," Mindu said as Sara and I took our seats at the table.

"Sorry, we were held up," Sara replied.

"Just don't let it happen again," Vensyr said, pushing his silver locket deep into his cloak.

Gibbs rolled his eyes. "Are you *effin'* serious?"

"He seems to be," Alex said.

"I am," said Vensyr. "Sara's the leader of the resistance, after all. Why do you care so much?"

"Oh, I don't know," Gibbs replied. "I guess I just don't see the point in us being here. Wasn't it *their* job to plan this mission?"

"Yes, but—"

"But nothing!" Gibbs yelled. "Vensyr, we've taken our precious time to help them! And what does the Kingslayer do? What does the *princess* do? They show up late. Not very professional for the leader of the resistance," he added, looking at Sara next to me. "Eh, Princess?"

"I've already apologized, Gibbs," Sara said angrily. "You can take it or leave it, but you will *not* talk to me with such disrespect. In fact, if you haven't anything nice to say, please refrain from saying anything at all."

"If you need to blame someone for us needing to be here, blame me," Vensyr told Gibbs, and it was quite obvious that he too was angry. "It was *I* who thought Sara and Mindu would be capable of planning the heist with two inexperienced soldiers. I guess I put too much faith in André, but can you blame me? For heaven's sake, he's only the *freakin'* Kingslayer!"

Gibbs slammed his fist on the table, looking angry enough to kill both Sara and Vensyr. I didn't know if I was just being paranoid, but I kept my left hand on my sword, just in case. After a moment, it became clear that he decided to fight with words, not arms, and that's when he turned to face Mindu. "What do *you* think, Wizard?" he asked, removing his bowler as he ran one hand through his thinning hair.

Mindu looked over his half-moon glasses. "Maybe they shouldn't have been late, but all in all, no harm's done. So, I implore you to forget it, as we *do* have more important things to discuss."

Gibbs was about to respond, but Sara stopped him from doing so. *"SILENCE!"* she roared, and the entire room fell silent. "I will not tolerate this, Gibbs. Your behavior is out of line, so you'd best keep your mouth shut! One more word may cost you your life!"

The elves and wizards of Alma Defa began talking amongst themselves, finding this argument between Sara and Gibbs interesting. But the debate was over (the argument finished), and I could tell by looking at her that Sara wasn't done talking.

"Besides," she continued, "I personally think Mindu was right in asking Vensyr to come. After all, he knows more about Tiberius than anyone else I know."

"Really?" I said in unison with Alex. I looked at Vensyr.

"Tiberius and I are first cousins,"[50] he said.

Never in a million years did I expect this revelation. But now that it was revealed, I had to admit it all made perfect sense. Vensyr *did* seem to know more about the Emperor than anyone else I knew. Part of me was eager to learn more (just like I was eager to win another chess tournament, or gain Excelsior already), but I could tell Vensyr didn't want to talk about it. Clearly, it brought back bad memories.

"You okay, Vensyr?" Sara asked after a moment.

Vensyr nodded. "I'm just sick of cleaning up after my cousin's mess," he replied. "Now, if you don't mind, I'd like to discuss the mission at hand."

"The floor's all yours," Sara told him.

On those words, Vensyr rolled out a map of the Imperial City. "There are *monstrous* obstacles," he said, looking at his men around the table and stressing the matters-of-fact

---

50 According to public records, Archibald Morfang (a lord on Michael Willington's Royal Council) was the maternal grandfather of Vensyr D'Artanian. It is also believed by historians that Lord Morfang was the paternal grandfather of the Black King Tiberius (A.K.A., Jennison Morfang), making General D'Artanian and King Tiberius first cousins.

There is some debate among scholars as to why the two men were on opposite sides of the Great Revolution, but one thing remains clear: their falling out ultimately led to Tiberius's rise to power.

to every tiny elf. "Dragonshade Wurms,[51] Sky Flails,[52] and then there's the city's largest gate."

But getting inside wasn't *my* concern, as it was Vensyr's. I took out Hugo's magic ring and showed it to him. "Why don't we just use this?" I asked. "That way, we can spend more time focusing on what to do once we're inside the city?"

Gibbs broke his silence. "You mean like stealing the key to the armory from the Black King while he sleeps?" he asked.

"That part had me concerned," Mindu admitted.

"For good reason. The one responsible for doing that is likely to end up dead. Ravana Valassaari will be close by, after all, and let's not forget that the armory is protected by a dozen Royal Guards. Am I *seriously* the only one sitting here who thinks this is a fool's errand, or do the rest of you just have a death wish or something?"

"We don't have much of a choice!" Alex insisted.

---

51 Dragonshade Wurms were shade-like dragon monsters, created by necromancers on the payroll of King Tiberius. Most of them were tens of thousands of feet tall and hundreds of feet wide, with rock-hard, black skin. During the reign of Tiberius, they were positioned around the walls of the Imperial City, making a siege nearly impossible.

52 Originally designed by Aldric Rookwood, Sky Flails are massive machines (flails chained to the ground) that are used to knock airships out of the sky with one swipe of their balls. In 1419, just before the Battle of Alma Defa, General Darius and his men mugged Rookwood and stole his designs so that his invention could be used to protect the Imperial City.

"Hundreds, maybe thousands of families have been torn apart by this abomination they're calling a war."

"It's your funeral," Gibbs replied.

Gibbs's words were troubling to me. Did he *really* plan on abandoning the resistance when they needed him most? Vensyr seemed to be under that impression.

He turned to face Gibbs immediately.

"You're not bailing on us, Gibbs. That's an order," he said. "But don't you worry. *I* will be the one to snatch the key so you don't have to get your *tender* hands dirty."

"And General," said one of Vensyr's knights, looking at Gibbs from across the table, "as you are aware, the knights of the resistance know what they're doing. Remember Operation Jabberwocky[53] a few weeks back? Did we not take care of the enemy before they even reached the city of Windull?"

---

53 In June of 1427, General Malakov led an army of Imperial Knights toward the city of Windull, hoping to destroy it as part of the Purge of Resistance. Their battle plan was to surround the city walls and wipe out Windull's inhabitants by brute force. However, before the Imperial Army could so much as reach the ruins of Tipp City, spies within their ranks alerted the resistance to the coming danger. In response, Vensyr D'Artanian, Aldric Rookwood, and Hugo von Salcroth devised a secret plan known as Operation Jabberwocky.

The mission was simple: locate the army and wipe them out before they reached the city of Windull. To achieve this end, the resistance used plague rats to infect the Imperial troop. With all but Malakov and a handful of others infected, the resistance easily overtook their foes. Only General Malakov and a couple others survived with their lives.

"Yes," Gibbs replied.

"We'll eliminate the enemy on this mission too, with just as much success," he added.

"So, is that all?" Alex asked, propping her dragonskin boots[54] onto the edge of the table.

Mindu looked at Vensyr's map of the Imperial City, scribbling notes on the blueprint of the palace walls with his feathered quill. "Let's see…. Vensyr's going to steal the key, his knights are going to take out the Royal Guards…." He paused, thinking. Then he looked at me and said, "*If General Valassaari or another general shows up, can you hold them off until you gain Excelsior?*"

"I'll do my best," I replied.

"Don't forget, the heist must be at night," Vensyr told Mindu, "while the palace sleeps."

"Of course. Never forgetting," Mindu said.

"Once we have Excelsior, how are we going to escape the palace?" I asked, the thought just occurring to me.

"Remember Marik Katsa?" Vensyr replied.

"You mean the metrosexual pirate who I could swear is in love with me?" I asked. "Yeah, I remember."

"I've asked him to take us to the Imperial City. How about we use your godfather's ring to teleport onto *The White Gauntlet* once we have the sword and make our getaway?"

---

54 Boots made from the hide of a dragon. They are worn mostly by the rich, because the leather is incredibly hard to come by.

I couldn't argue with that idea.

Mindu handed me his Bynch Book. "Take this," he said. "Vensyr already has one, as he *is* a general. You two will need to communicate somehow if something goes wrong."

"Don't you need it though?" I asked.

"Not at all, since I will be with Marik, overseeing the operation onboard *The White Gauntlet*. If something goes wrong, use that book and contact Marik with it. Since he's got one just like it, you'll be able to contact him with yours. I will then come to the palace and resolve whatever issues come up, but please avoid calling on me, since a duel with the Black King could result in my death."

"But your wheelchair..." Alex pointed out. "You're hardly capable of moving fast enough to aid us in time."

"Not if Marik carries me to your location," Mindu replied, twirling his wand through the fingers of his left hand.

The elves and wizards of Alma Defa rose to acknowledge the end of our meeting. Now, I knew what would be required of me. So did Sara, who seemed ready for what came next. But I could tell she now had her mind away from the meeting, likely because she wanted to spend one last day with me and Alex. After all, the mission would soon be our focus.

9

THE MEETING HALL at headquarters shook on its foundations, and that second, Mindu's wheelchair began moving until Alex grabbed it. I could hear women screaming outside. I looked out the nearest window; then, I saw black airships, floating above the elfish city. Vensyr and Gibbs rose from their seats. Both of them drew their weapons.

What's going on? I wondered.

I stood to join them; Alex and Sara did as well. After a moment, an elf with a large cut across his tunic entered the meeting hall. His sword was drawn, and both his hands were covered in blood. Clearly, whatever was going on outside wasn't good. Vensyr approached the elf with Gibbs, and to me, he looked full of worry.

"Mikus…" Mindu said, falling silent as Vensyr cleared his throat to speak.

"What's going on outside?" Vensyr asked. The meeting hall shook again.

The elf sheathed his sword and sat where Alex had

previously been sitting. Breathing heavily for a moment, he didn't say a word; then, looking at Vensyr and then at me, he cupped his hands and started to talk.

"It's the Imperial Knights," he said. "They're everywhere, attacking the city. They want *him,*" he added, pointing at me with one finger. "I think someone's betrayed us. How *else* could they know he's here, let alone remove the shields that were protecting the island?"[55]

"Which generals are leading them?" Sara asked as several wizards and elves entered the meeting hall.

"Magnus Morfang and Ravana Valassaari," said a Wizard of the Third Order. "I might've seen General Darius as well."

"You did," said a sudden, familiar voice, "and Morfang and Valassaari are both headed in this direction. If we expect to keep the Kingslayer safe, we better move him to *The White Gauntlet* as soon as possible."

I looked to see who had spoken, and at once, Marik Katsa entered the hall with the lovely Eelra by his side. Both

---

55 In the aftermath of the Battle of Alma Defa, the resistance put an Elypsian Stone onto a pedestal in the highest room of their headquarters. That way, they could place magic shields over the island that were strong enough to ward off any attack from the Empire.

For over eight years, the Elypsian Stone was in place; however, on July 28th, 1427, the stone was stolen by an unknown traitor, making it possible for the Empire to attack.

pirates looked exhausted, as if they'd already faced several Imperial Knights on their way to headquarters.

"'Ello, *Sweety!*" Marik said jokingly to me.

"Marik Katsa!" Eelra spat. "Now *isn't* the time for that!"

"Right," he said, taking off his triangle hat in his usual feminine manner. Now, he turned his attention toward the elves and wizards in the meeting hall. "Head for the fortress city of Alexandretta," he told them. "Do whatever you have to, but the island *must* be evacuated. If you have to, board my airship. I'm heading straight for Alexandretta once Bellbrook gains Excelsior. Just get off the island, because I'm certain they plan on blowing it out of the sky." Marik looked at Vensyr and Gibbs, and to me, it looked like he wanted to kiss one of them. "Generals, you're lucky Lord Salcroth and General Rookwood were paying attention to the skies and contacted me. Otherwise, you and the Kingslayer would be *screwed!*"

It wasn't long before the elves and wizards that were present began teleporting out of the room, taking on the form of dissipating smoke.[56] Soon, Marik and Eelra drew their flintlock pistols, and Vensyr grabbed my arm, escorting me out of headquarters for my own protection. Next thing I knew, I was walking down an alleyway as bombs dropped and fires rose from the cobblestone streets. Luckily,

---

56 When a wizard or magic savvy non-wizard uses a teleportation spell, they take the form of dissipating smoke.

the resistance aided me, which meant I was safe for the time being.

It felt like any moment could be my last. I kept expecting Magnus or Ravana to appear out of nowhere, but at the moment, they were nowhere in sight.

"Look!" Sara said, pointing toward the sky.

That's when I saw it.

The White Gauntlet was floating high above every building in Alma Defa, about six miles off in the distance. It appeared to be dodging cannon fire from enemy ships, but it was also returning fire as well. Once I stood onboard Marik's ironclad vessel, hopefully I'd be safe from danger. But I still had a road to walk, and that path led me deeper into the threat of the Imperial Army. It seemed like everywhere I turned, there were Imperial Knights trying to arrest me. But that was okay because I was aided by the best soldiers I'd ever seen, and nearly all of them—Sara, Marik, and Vensyr to name a few—were prepared to defend the Kingslayer, even if it cost them their lives.

Suddenly, two clouds of black smoke came barreling towards us out of the sky. At first, I thought they were cannonballs, but as they landed in the cobblestone streets without crashing into anything, I knew this couldn't be true. Soon, I realized they were Magnus and Ravana, armed and ready to kill. But matters only got worse from there. Nearly a dozen Imperial Knights came around the bend, entering into the alley in which we stood. Needless to say, I was in trouble: I was pinned between the knights who hunted me and the walls of the alleyway.

"Surrender, Bellbrook!" Ravana yelled, aiming her wand at me.

"Give me one reason why I should!" I said at once.

"André, no!" Alex whispered, but I wasn't going to listen.

Sara stepped forward as Vensyr pulled me to the back of our party. "If you want him, come and claim him!" she said, drawing her pistol and activating its spring-loaded bayonet.

Immediately, Vensyr, Gibbs, Marik, and Eelra opened fire at the Imperial Knights, just as Sara stabbed two or three of them with her flintlock's bayonet. Some of them died because of these attacks, while others were not as easy to kill. Still, Ravana grew angry due to the deaths of her fallen men. She moved forward to engage our party (ready to take out as many of us as she could), but Mindu wasn't having any of it.

He took a finely-crafted, ivory wand out of his vest's inner-pocket. "No you don't, Valassaari!" Mindu zapped a red beam of light at Ravana;[57] she wasn't prepared. At once, her wand caught fire, forcing her to drop it before the blaze could singe her fingers. Alex rolled Mindu forward on his

---

57 *Deathfyre:* A spell capable of killing anyone who touches its searing hot flame. It is also a useful tool when it comes to destroying wands and other weapons.

command; meanwhile, Mindu aimed his wand at Ravana and said, "My name is Rubin Mindu. I am a wizard: one far beyond your caliber, Valassaari. Now, why don't you let us go before someone gets hurt?"

Ravana hesitated, going up against the Fifth Wizard.

"What's wrong?" Magnus demanded.

"He's a Wizard of the Fifth Order…" she replied.

"I thought we killed them all."

"Apparently not," Ravana said, looking at her men. "Kill him!" she said in a panic. *"Do it now!"*

"I've killed better soldiers than them, Valassaari," Mindu said. At once, he unleashed a wave of blue fire from his wand, scorching the remaining knights that followed Magnus and Ravana.[58] Soon, only the generals remained standing. "Now," Mindu continued, aiming his wand at Magnus and Ravana, "if I were you, I'd let us go."

"You're going to pay for that!" Ravana said, taking out her pistol a moment later.

BANG! Mindu disarmed her with a swipe of his wand.[59] "If you let us go, I'll let you live. There's no need to be foolish!" he said. Magnus aimed his gun at Mindu (preparing to fire), but the wizard then disarmed him as well. "Not a wise

---

58 *Incintricus:* A fire spell designed to burn its target. When it is cast by a fully-trained Fifth Wizard, this spell is capable of killing multiple soldiers at once: scorching them from the inside out.

59 *Disarmithyss:* A spell that is capable of knocking a weapon or object out of its owner's hand(s).

move, Morfang," Mindu told him. "Now, this is your last chance. Let us go, or die!"

"Let's go, Mother," Magnus said, taking Ravana along by the wrist; then, he looked me dead in the eyes. "Run to your precious airship, Bellbrook," he said. "We will follow you wherever you go. *There is no escape!*" They took on the form of their teleportation spells. The next thing I knew, they were headed for the largest airship in the sky.

"Take out Hugo's ring," Vensyr said, "before they can circle back. We'll grab onto you and teleport together."

"I agree," Marik said, looking at his ship in the sky. "My ship isn't far."

10

MY BODY SLAMMED down on the polished wood floor of *The White Gauntlet*'s main deck. I pulled myself up, releasing my hold over Alex and Sara, *and* everyone else in our party as they scrambled to their feet. A moment later, I pulled Hugo's ring off my finger and dropped it into one of the pockets of my waistcoat; then, looking at the main deck, I saw the men of Marik's crew. Most of them were armed with swords and wands, plus flintlock pistols that were locked and loaded. I knew it at once: they would protect the Kingslayer, no matter what the cost.

On Marik's command, *The White Gauntlet* started to move. And before long, I saw the ships of the Imperial Fleet, dropping bombs endlessly on Alma Defa. I could only imagine how the families of the sky-bound island felt that moment, seeing their home destroyed. In some ways, it was like the attack on Willowbrook all over again. Only, it wasn't Luke who was murdered this time, and this time I was seeing the massacre through a different set of eyes.

I made my way toward the edge of *The White Gauntlet* as Alex and Sara followed. As we stood there (not far from Vensyr and Gibbs), I could see many Imperial airships, firing upon the spells and enchantments that kept the island air-bound. When the strongest spells were broken, the island crashed into the ocean below. A massive tidal wave then rose up from the water, which was likely to hit the nearest coastline.

Sara wrapped her arms around me. "Hold me," she said. She was trembling. Clearly, she was scared for both my life, and her own.

"Marik," Vensyr said, approaching the sky pirate. "This is your airship. What do you suggest we do?"

"We'll have to outrun them," Marik replied.

But the task of fleeing the Imperial Fleet was easier said than done. There had to be at least nine airships after *The White Gauntlet,* all of which were bigger and faster than Marik's ironclad vessel. Cannonballs came at us from every direction, but Marik and his crew were ready. *The White Gauntlet* dodged these attacks, returning fire and knocking two enemy ships right out of the sky. As the ships went down, many Imperial Knights escaped, using broomsticks and teleportation spells in order to remain air-bound. Among them was General Darius, flying toward *The White Gauntlet* with several of his men.

Soon, they would try and burst its balloon in an attempt to bring us down.

"We have to stop them!" Sara said, drawing her flintlock pistol.

She fired off three rounds and sent a couple Imperial Knights falling into the ocean below. Vensyr's men and Alex joined in on the attack, and Mindu made use of his wand. Unfortunately, not all of them were killed. Soon, Darius arrived onboard *The White Gauntlet* with three of his knights remaining.

"Surrender, Bellbrook!" he yelled. "Simply fleeing the Empire is treason. Do you *really* want Tiberius to have you killed?"

"He already wants me dead!" I said, taking out my sword.

Darius looked angry. "Running is treason! If you don't—"

BANG! Mindu fired a red stream of light from his wand, sending Darius flying off the edge of *The White Gauntlet*.[60] At once, the general became like a puff of dissipating smoke, and he was gone. Vensyr and his knights then opened fire upon the men who followed Darius. When they were killed, I looked at the Imperial Fleet and saw them losing speed. Could we possibly escape them? It sure seemed like it, *if* we could evade their fastest ship.

---

60 *Strikklys:* A basic spell that knocks over its target.

But the Empire's command ship[61] was directly behind us, which was bad news if we hoped to escape. This ship alone had the crew of *The White Gauntlet* completely out-gunned. If Magnus and Ravana wanted it done, they could have us knocked right out of the sky.

Luckily for us, however, Marik had a plan.

"Mindu," he said, removing his triangle hat as he approached the old Fifth Wizard, "can you cast a Cloaking Spell and make the ship invisible?"

"Yes, but what will that accomplish?" Mindu asked, leaning back in his wheelchair. "Those onboard the command ship will see me do it. They'll still know where we are."

"Not if we blur their vision. I'll be right back. I have an idea."

At once, Marik went below deck. Then a few seconds later, I heard him yelling something to his men. The next thing I knew, several cannons below deck fired at the Empire's command ship, and mushrooms of smoke appeared at each point of impact.

Marik returned to the main deck and looked at Mindu.

"It's time," he said. "Make the ship invisible."

It was right on these words that I realized what Marik was up to. The impact of the cannonballs upon the Empire's

---

61 A type of airship that leads an entire fleet. During the Great Revolution, an airship of this class would've been controlled or captained by Magnus Morfang, Ravana Valassaari, or another high-ranking general of the Imperial Knights.

command ship had smothered the vessel in a cloud of thick, black smoke: one the Imperial Knights couldn't see through for the life of them. Now, with their ship covered in smoke and our own about to be invisible, it was going to look like we'd gotten away.

"All right," Mindu replied, aiming his wand toward the edge of *The White Gauntlet*, "let's make our escape."

And the ship was invisible like a breath of fresh air.

11

"It's beautiful," Sara said.

From the deck of *The White Gauntlet,* I watched with Sara, Vensyr, and Alex as the skyline of the Imperial City appeared over the edge of the horizon. It was a beautiful city (like Sara said), with many white buildings, a grand wall protecting the boundaries, and a port for many ships of the sea. Just seeing the ancient city made me realize how out of place Tiberius was on its throne. It belonged to a real king (a *White* King),[62] like Michael Willington before him.

I looked at Sara, crying. I couldn't blame her for being emotional, because all her life, she'd been forced to stay clear of the city she called her home. Now that she was back (and could therefore see it), it must've been all she'd dreamt about and more. To Sara, this mission was more than just a turning point in the war. It was also her homecoming.

---

62 A White King is a ruler who the church considers righteous in the ways of Redisy. By contrast, a Black King (like Tiberius) is a ruler who the church considers evil. Not every king in Isobellian history has held such titles.

"I can't wait to go inside," she said.

But it would be awhile before that happened. The sun was still out, and if we stuck to the plan, we'd only teleport inside once the city had gone to sleep. "Aren't we supposed to wait until nightfall?" I asked, looking at Vensyr.

Vensyr nodded. "You're right; we've come too early," he agreed. "Marik?" He motioned the sky pirate in our direction.

"What yah need, *Sweety-pie!?*" Marik asked.

"Take us to the Evergreen Forest," Vensyr said. "It should only be a few miles, I think. Landing the ship there will give us cover while we wait for nightfall."

"I'll have it done in a *jiffy!*" Marik replied.

Mindu rolled forward in his wheelchair. "Do the three of you have your Bynch Books?" he asked. At once, I pulled the Bynch Book out of my pocket; then, out came Marik's and Vensyr's as well. Mindu looked pleased. "Vensyr, André… keep in touch with one another while the mission is under-way. If something goes wrong, contact Marik onboard *The White Gauntlet.* I will handle things then."

***

When night fell, Vensyr readied his knights for the mission at hand. Meanwhile, Sara, Alex, Gibbs, and I stood ready to go: battle garments on, heavily armed. Naturally, I was nervous of the moments to come, but I knew my anxiety wouldn't last. Very soon, Excelsior would be mine.

"Lower the ship near the gates," Vensyr told Marik.

When this was done, our small party jumped out of *The White Gauntlet* and rested on a hill. Mindu then cast a second Cloaking Spell over the airship,[63] leaving us to the mission at hand. Just like Vensyr said, there were massive obstacles protecting the city: Dragonshade Wurms on the ground, Sky Flails in the sky. These obstacles made it clear why I needed Hugo's magic ring in the first place. To go without would make it impossible to reach the city alive, let alone break into the palace and steal Excelsior.

I reached for the ring inside my pocket. As I did, everyone grabbed on tight so we could teleport into the city together. Soon, we were standing in the middle of a deserted street corner, looking around for Imperial Knights. At the moment, none were in sight.

Sara drew out her pistol and said, "Everyone take out your weapons. None of us are safe here."

Everyone took out their weapons on Sara's suggestion. I drew my sword; Vensyr, his men, *and* the arrogant Gibbs took out their flintlock pistols; and Alex brandished an ivory wand as to protect herself. Together, we moved into an alleyway, hidden by the shadows of the night. There was an entire sky-line of buildings blocking my view as we reached the Royal

---

63 *Invisicus Totalum:* An illusion-type enchantment that can make a person or object invisible. When cast upon a large object like an airship, the person casting it usually needs to be a fully-trained wizard.

District,[64] but I could still make out the Imperial Palace off in the distance.

For about fifteen minutes, we moved toward the castle, killing men on patrol when necessary. As we arrived, there were about a dozen Imperial Knights, guarding the palace doors. Bartimus Rothenheim was the man who led them. When I saw him, I knew Tiberius wasn't taking security risks lightly. Rothenheim was, after all, the general who led the attack that ended the Fifth Order.

Vensyr signaled for his men to act, and at once, they moved forward and shot down several Imperial Knights. Vensyr shot Rothenheim right in the head (before the man had a chance to act); then, he ripped the key to the palace doors from his dead hands. Seeing them act so quickly, I knew Vensyr's men had told Gibbs the truth. The knights of the resistance *did* know what they were doing. It was no wonder why Operation Jabberwocky had been so successful.

Vensyr handed the key to one of his knights; then, into a padlock it went.

We were in! Finally, after weeks of being hunted and being pressured to come out of hiding, I was in the Imperial Palace: the stronghold of the same Black King I'd been so afraid of crossing to begin with. I was closer now than ever before to

---

64 The city's main housing district for the king and his knights. It is home to the Imperial Palace, plus other government buildings that were not used during Tiberius's reign.

avenging my parents and Luke. All I had to do now was gain Excelsior, and maybe I could avenge them that very evening.

Sara holstered her gun and brandished a wand, conjuring a light to brighten the dark corridor.[65] "You ready for this?" she asked, looking at me.

I nodded. "Yeah," I said.

Vensyr approached me and Sara. "I'll meet you guys at the armory. I'm going to steal that key." He looked me dead in the eyes. "We both have Bynch Books in case something goes wrong. I suggest we use them. Keep an eye on yours."

Again, I nodded, this time at Vensyr. Once he was gone, I looked at the rest of our party and said, "I guess that's our cue to begin our search for the armory."

"Agreed," Gibbs said, cocking his pistol. "Let's go."

***

For twenty-five minutes (or so it seemed), our party searched for the armory that held Excelsior. We moved down a single corridor and up one winding staircase, using the map that Vensyr provided to guide our way. Sara pointed at it, illuminating the blueprint of the castle walls with the light at the tip of her wand. From what I could tell, the armory was in the castle's highest tower (not far from the airship docking bay). When we arrived there, I knew my sense of direction was accurate.

---

65 *Illuminatus:* A basic spell that can light up a small area. It gives the wand the same function as a torch lit with fire.

There was just one problem: several guards watched over the armory's iron doors. But we had to get past them. If we didn't, the Empire would never be freed, and Luke and my parents would never be avenged.

"Fire!" Sara yelled at Vensyr's men; then, a general of the Imperial Knights yelled, "Fire!"

Immediately, members from both sides fired upon their enemy, shooting bullets and flinging spells. I managed to bounce a red jet of light back at its caster with the edge of my sword,[66] when Alex and Sara pulled out their pistols and fired them, just like Vensyr's men. Six Imperial Knights were left. I charged at them with the rest of the party, cutting my sword into the heart of General Boris. When this was done, I looked around, seeing that every Imperial Knight had been killed.

"Let's move their bodies," Sara said as I returned my sword to its sheath. "It'd be nice to have a clear floor when Vensyr gets here."

But Vensyr's return would be more complicated than I originally thought. Just as the words left Sara's lips, I felt something vibrating in my pocket. That's when I pulled out my Bynch Book, opening its pages to see a message from Vensyr that read:

I have the key, but Tiberius has woken. When I arrive, we must hurry.

---

66 *Strikklys:* A basic spell that knocks over its target.

VENSYR'S INTERLUDE

July 29th, 1427

Since leaving Issylot, Jocelyn and I watched as the rolling hills of the Gililands passed by our compartment window. We were aboard *The Runaway Express,* which was fitting since we were fleeing the country. If we were seen, we were as good as dead. But we wouldn't stay on the train long since we were nearing the Empire's border.

"There's been an attack on Alma Defa," Jocelyn said, turning the pages of *The Isobellian Times.*

Of course, this wasn't a surprise. Tiberius ruled the Empire with an iron fist. If there *was* an attack (like Jocelyn said), then all it meant was that the Emperor was now beyond all redemption.

"Vensyr, are you sure it's okay to leave now, given what is going on?" Jocelyn asked.

"It's not like we've got a better choice. Besides, my clone will take care of things in my stead."

I looked at Jocelyn, combing her fingers through her curly red hair. To be honest, she looked upset by the news of Alma Defa, but this was nothing compared to what we'd already faced together. Since our marriage began, Tiberius had tried to tear us apart. But we were still alive, still in love, and we would soon be out of my cousin's reach. As the storybooks say, our tale had a happy ending.

I was just glad to be putting this war behind us.

"How long until we cross the border?" Jocelyn asked.

"'Bout fifteen minutes," I replied, checking my pocket watch to see the time.

"Good," Jocelyn said; then, she looked back down at the daily newspaper.

PART THREE

The Battle of Lyonisis
July-August 1427

12

I STARTED TO panic. Tiberius—the one person who wanted me dead—was coming to face me. While it was true that I'd have to face him eventually, I'd be lying if I said I wanted that to happen today. *If only he'd remained asleep…* then I could've escaped the Imperial City—armed with Excelsior—without much trouble. But now I had reason to worry, and how could I not have been? It's not every day you meet someone who wants to see you killed.

I still had my Bynch Book opened up as Vensyr's men began moving dead bodies away from the armory's doorway. *I need to tell Marik,* I thought, so I pulled an old pencil from my waistcoat and wrote him a message that read:

Tiberius is awake.

We know, Marik replied a minute later. *We're preparing for the worst as I write this to you. If Tiberius finds you, send red sparks from the tip of your wand out of the nearest window. That way, we'll know where to find you.*

Sara walked up to me. "What's wrong?" she asked, looking at the cleared floor in front of the armory.

I didn't know what to say. How could I *possibly* tell her?

"Tell me," she said.

I drew in a deep breath and said, "Tiberius is awake." I held up my Bynch Book. "Vensyr just told me."

It was just as I'd predicted: panic filled the room. The only one in our party who seemed unafraid was Gibbs. But then again, he didn't have much to lose. Gibbs didn't care about anyone except himself.

I grabbed Sara by the hand and reached for her chest, dropping my Bynch Book in an effort to put her mind at ease. "It's okay," I said. "I just heard from Marik. If Tiberius finds us, he said to send red sparks out of the nearest window. That way, they'll know where to find us."

"Why can't we just teleport onto *The White Gauntlet* if he finds us?" Alex asked. I pulled my Bynch Book off the floor. "Just grab Excelsior; then, *poof*, we're gone?"

"It's not that simple," Sara said. "There are enchantments protecting the armory, so we can't just teleport close to it at free will. To do so (even *with* Hugo's ring at our disposal), we'd have to break every rule of magic known to man. You'd be hard pressed to do that, Alex, even *with* the gods on your side."

"Sara's got a point," came a familiar voice behind me. "But lucky for us, it won't come to that."

It was Vensyr. He tossed me the key to the armory, looking as if he'd gone through twist and turn just to escape Tiberius. My heart was racing as I considered what I was about to do. It was treason. If I did this, there was no going back. But I had to do it. It was the only way I would survive the war, let alone avenge both Luke and my parents. So, I inserted the key into the padlock of the armory doorway; then, with a turn of the key, I heard a loud *click,* and the door slid open.

Great awe overcame me as I looked at all the items in the armory. Most of the Relics of Redisy were there (some of which I didn't expect to see),[67] but Excelsior was not as easy to find.

"Where do you think it is?" I asked, looking at Sara and then at Vensyr. Neither of them seemed to know.

But after a moment, we found it.

It was on a shelf (not far from a portrait of Sr. Avril the Lionheart),[68] tucked behind various weapons of iron

---

67 According to written documents, there were only two Relics of Redisy missing from the Black King's armory the night Excelsior was stolen. One was the Immortality Ring (which Tiberius wore at all times for his protection), and the other was the Everlasting Flame (which was never in the Emperor's possession at all).

68 Sr. Avril the Lionheart (also called St. Avril the Wise) was a legendary knight living around the time of St. Aramara. He was a Member of Redisy, a guardian of the Relics of Redisy, and was one of the few men who founded the Church of Redisy 40 days after St. Aramara's untimely death.

and brass. The blade was like nothing I'd ever seen before: a beautiful sword with a red florescent glow. Seeing the sword, taking it into my hands.... That's when I realized it was true. I *was* the Kingslayer. I had chosen to believe it before that moment, but now my destiny couldn't be denied by anyone.

"Well done, Kingslayer," Vensyr said with a smile. "Our salvation has come at last."

Sara drew close to me. "I'm so proud of you," she said as I strapped Excelsior to my belt. "My hero..." she added as her voice trailed off.

Suddenly, I heard three solid claps, as if someone behind me was cheering me on. "Good, Andreas. *Good!*" said an unknown, cold voice.

Tiberius entered the armory, taking out his flintlock pistol. He was easily the most frightening man I'd ever met, with jet-black hair and an eyepatch over his left socket. His good eye looked at me with absolute hatred, and that's when I realized why only the resistance dared to cross him. If anyone did, he had no problem killing them off.

"Tiberius—" I began, stopping dead as the Black King cocked his pistol.

"Be quiet," he demanded.

St. Avril is credited for the creation of the hierarchy of clergymen (bishops, archbishops, cardinals, and the single High Bishop). In fact, many church scholars believe Avril was the first High Bishop to run the church until his death in the year 64.

"You will *not* command the Kingslayer," Vensyr said.

Tiberius fired a warning shot into the ceiling of the armory; meanwhile, Alex fired red sparks from her wand out of the nearest window.[69] I looked at Alex, smiling at me. With any luck, Marik and Mindu would be along any minute.

"It's been awhile, Cousin," Tiberius said to Vensyr, cocking his pistol for the second time. "*Finally,* I can pay you back for all that you've put me through."

"Can't we talk about this?" Vensyr asked.

"*We* won't be talking at all; *you* did most of the talking when we were kids. Not anymore. *I* am in charge now, not *you! I* am the Black King, and *you* are just a puppet who's been manipulated by the resistance leadership."

"Lies—"

"*Did I tell you to speak!?*" Tiberius yelled. "*No one* better speak until spoken to!"

Tiberius aimed his gun at Vensyr's head.

"I'm going to kill you now," he said. "First you join the resistance, then you help the Kingslayer in gaining Excelsior? *Does your treachery know no bounds!?* This here proves it. You're too dangerous to be left alive. Therefore, it

---

69 *Flarkyss:* A fire-based signaling spell, designed to inform others of its caster's location. This sorcery is generally harmless, unless it is cast by a fully-trained Fifth Wizard.

is only fitting that I—His *Imperial Majesty*—sentence you to death!"

"Jenison, *no!*"

"Goodbye, *Cousin!*" Tiberius yelled.

Tiberius fired his pistol right into Vensyr's skull. Sara and Alex both screamed as Vensyr's body hit the floor, a moment before Tiberius reloaded his gun. I couldn't believe what had just happened. The world as I knew it was over, because another innocent soul was gone. Originally, I had thought Vensyr would help Sara in rebuilding the Empire once the war was over.

Now I knew that wasn't going to happen.

"He got his just reward," Tiberius said, now aiming his pistol at me. "Vensyr and I go way back. We're kinsman, you see. The man put me through the worst kind of humiliation, so I had every right to dispose of him, despite what you may believe."

"He told me you were cousins," I said, pulling Excelsior from its sheath, just in case Tiberius wanted to fight, "which explains how he knew your real name is Jenison."

Tiberius said nothing.

"Look, you can justify it however you want, but *nothing* gives you the right to murder."

"*Murder?* It's justice! If only you knew what he did to me."

"Tell me then."

"Let's just say my family was dysfunctional," Tiberius said.

"It doesn't take a genius to figure that out," I replied. "What could Vensyr *possibly* have done to make you hate him so much?"

"Before I get to that," Tiberius said, "there's something else you need to know first."

"Spill it then," I insisted.

At once, Tiberius began to tell his life story. "When I was a teen, I fell in love," he said. "It was Ravana Valassaari, who like Vensyr, was my first cousin. Unfortunately, Vensyr found out about our incestuous relationship. He then told our grandfather—a very wealthy and influential lord on the Royal Council[70]—everything. Needless to say, I was disowned and disinherited, and Ravana had to spend the rest of her teenage years with a *freakin'* scarlet letter on her chest!"

"That's not Vensyr's fault!" Sara said. "He didn't know your grandfather would—"

"*Hold your tongue!*" Tiberius yelled, and the whole room fell silent. "Vensyr may not have been the one who ultimately disowned me, but he's the only reason the entire town of Kul Jilra[71] found out about me and Ravana. *That* is

---

70 Archibald Morfang, as revealed in footnote 50.
71 The hometown of the Black King Tiberius (A.K.A., Jenison Morfang), plus Vensyr D'Artanian and Ravana Valassaari.

why I killed him. It's justice for all the humiliation he put me through!"

"But a man is dead now because of you!" I replied.

"And I should care why?" I was speechless. He continued. "Of course, I have to admit that part of me *is* thankful for Vensyr's betrayal. After all, if it wasn't for him, I'd never have gained access to the Relics of Redisy, nor would I be sitting on the Imperial Throne."

"That makes no sense," Alex said.

"Then allow me to explain. The moment I was disowned, I lost everything. Ravana, my home, *everything* but the clothes on my back. I think it goes without saying that I had no one to turn to. Anyone who so much as put a roof over my head would've had my grandfather to answer to. The only exception, of course, was the Church of Redisy. They took me in, clothed me, and fed me."

"You're *not* a Member of Redisy!" Sara said, looking completely appalled.

But Tiberius had proof. Just then, he pulled back the sleeve of his gun-bearing arm, revealing the Mark of Redisy that was branded to his wrist. "Believe me now?" he asked.

"You're not fit to be a Member of Redisy!" I said.

"That's *your* opinion, but I know my righteous calling. Why else do you think I've been collecting the Relics of Redisy all these years? It is my goal to unite the world under a single government, led by a single religion. And with the

Relics, I will make that dream a reality. According to scripture, when all seven are brought together, they can give the one who wields them the power to be a god among men."

"Everyone knows that," Sara said. "The Relics have only been used that way once, and it took a thousand men just to slay the warlord who possessed them all."[72]

"That's the power I'm trying to obtain," Tiberius said, "and I'm certain the gods want me to have that power. Why else would they allow me to gain six of the seven Relics? *It has to be their will!* And once I have all seven, I will unite the world under a single creed! That's why I have no problem killing you off, Bellbrook, *if* you don't give me that *bloody* sword!"

"Do you *really* think you can blame Vensyr for your rise to power?" I asked, ignoring Tiberius's demand.

"I do," he replied. "After all, is he not the one who led me to the church *and* the Imperial Throne? Without his betrayal, I wouldn't be in control of the Relics of Redisy, and I sure as hell wouldn't have killed your parents. *That's right, Bellbrook!* If not for Vensyr, both your parents would still be alive!"

Tiberius seemed finished with his speech. Some of his story made perfect sense, while the rest of it confused me to no end. Did he *really* think he could blame Vensyr for the fate of my parents? Yes, Vensyr led Tiberius to his eventual

---

72 Pius the Great, the Black King of the Heroshian Empire.

rise to power, but that didn't make him my parents' killer. Tiberius was just toying with my mind, trying to make me blame Vensyr instead. His little mind games didn't work, but why was he so ready to blame Vensyr when their grandfather was left unmentioned?

I decided to address the issue.

"If you had to kill someone for all that you've been through," I asked, "why didn't you just kill off your grandfather? After all, wasn't he the one who disinherited you?"

"Oh, I killed him years ago.[73] But now that Vensyr's gone, justice is finally done. Now I just have to kill *you*, Bellbrook. *That* will be the icing on the cake that is my life!"

"Icing on the cake?" I repeated, completely disgusted. "*What kind of monster are you!?* Is power and revenge all that you're living for?"

"What?"

Tiberius looked shocked. Of all the things I could've said, nothing had surprised him like this. But the time for talk was over. He looked at me with hatred now, his finger on the trigger of his gun. He was about to fire.

Or so I thought.

A red jet of light shot into the armory, knocking

---

73 Archibald Morfang and his family were murdered on September 5th, 1403 (the day after Vensyr D'Artanian and his wife Jocelyn were married). Vensyr and Jocelyn were the only members of the family to have survived this massacre, since they were away on their honeymoon when the murders took place.

Tiberius off his feet.[74] Suddenly, Marik appeared, carrying Mindu in his arms.

"Let's go!" Mindu said, gripping on tightly to his wand.

Everyone fled the armory on Mindu's command, but soon the Black King was up again. Yelling and screaming, Tiberius shot and killed two of Vensyr's men. His fury knew no equal. He wanted to kill off our entire party.

We ran through the nearest corridor and down one flight of stairs. Once we reached the ground floor, Gibbs took the lead. Still grasping his pistol, he led us to the castle's main entrance. But as I stepped forward to open the palace doors, Gibbs turned around and aimed his gun at me.

"*Freeze!*" he yelled. "Don't move or I'll put a bullet in you!"

I was shocked. Yes, Gibbs was one of the most difficult generals I had to deal with. Part of me even wondered why he was in the resistance. But why was he threatening to kill me?

Tiberius entered the hall, flanked by Darius and several Royal Guards. "Very good, Gibbs," he said, throwing Gibbs a sack of gold. "Here's the rest I owe you," he added. "Nice work."

"*What is the meaning of this!?*" I demanded.

"I'm just doing as I've been paid to do," Gibbs replied, stowing the gold inside his waistcoat.

---

74 *Strikklys:* A basic spell that knocks over its target.

"What reason could you possibly have to—?"

"—to betray you?" he said. "Look, I've lost family in this war. *On both sides!* At this point, I honestly don't give a flying crap who wins. I just want the war to be over. That's why I agreed to take Tiberius's money, infiltrate Alma Defa, and report on resistance dealings."

"*You* betrayed us at Alma Defa?" Sara asked.

"Well, it certainly wasn't the Mother Creator," Gibbs replied, cocking his pistol.

Darius and the Royal Guards drew closer. Any moment, they would try to arrest me.

Tiberius looked at Sara and said, "Looks like you've misplaced your trust, Highness. Quite the failure, in my ever so humble opinion."

His words seemed to really hurt Sara. "How could you betray us?" she asked, looking at Gibbs.

"Because I was never on your side to begin with," he said.

"It's treason then," Sara said, aiming her gun at Gibbs. She was preparing to fire. "I'm going to kill—"

Gibbs fired his pistol before Sara was able to. Immediately, Sara hit the floor as blood came from her wounded side; meanwhile, Tiberius, Darius, and their men prepared to engage our party. The entire room was in an uproar as Mindu sent Gibbs flying into a corner (killing him by blunt-force trauma),[75] and I rushed to Sara's side (making sure she was all right). Unfortunately, Sara was *not* all right. Gibbs's bullet had penetrated her skin, after all. The wound wasn't bad enough to kill her, but now she was unable to defend herself.

"André…" she moaned, reaching out one hand for me while holstering her pistol with the other. She was in a lot of pain. There was no way I could duel Tiberius with Sara in need of medical attention, so I sheathed Excelsior and lifted her up.

BANG! Mindu slammed Tiberius and Darius into a corner.[76]

"Darius, where the devil are Magnus and Ravana!?" Tiberius yelled as the two men scrambled to their feet.

"Is *The White Gauntlet* still invisible?" I asked Mindu.

"No," he said. "When you make it outside, you should be able to see the airship. It should be in range of Hugo's ring by now."

Again, Tiberius fired his gun at members of our party, but Mindu protected them by conjuring a powerful, magical shield.[77] The Fifth Wizard then swished his wand

---

75 *Strikklys:* A basic spell that knocks over its target.

76 *Telékotyss:* A telekinetic spell capable of knocking over its target when used by a Wizard of the Fifth Order.

77 *Shyldig Totalum:* An entry-level enchantment that serves as a protective barrier from any oncoming attack, magical or otherwise. When cast by a Wizard of the Fifth Order, this spell can be unusually powerful.

around, turning it into a whip of thorns so he could face Tiberius himself.[78] This was just the distraction I needed, so without hesitation, I charged the palace doors and made it safely outside.

I looked into the sky, seeing *The White Gauntlet* just out of reach from the Sky Flails. I looked at Sara in my arms as she looked right back, grabbing on tight. I pulled Hugo's ring from my pocket. The ring was in range of *The White Gauntlet*, I had Excelsior…. It was time to teleport to safety.

"We're safe," I told Sara. "Everything's going to be okay." And with that, I slipped on Hugo's ring, and we were on *The White Gauntlet* a moment later.

The mission was a success.

---

78 *Battlethorne:* A combat sorcery, designed to turn a wand into a close-range weapon.

13

Sara moaned in pain as I scrambled to my feet to check on her wounded side. Unfortunately, blood had drenched the fabrics of her battle garments by the time everyone else made it onboard *The White Gauntlet*. Vensyr's men rushed to Sara's side. This was good, because I didn't know how to medically heal someone's injuries. This was a job for a doctor, which I was not. If only I could've helped her. But like Alex, I was forced to watch Vensyr's men, helpless as they tended to her injuries.

Will she be okay? I wondered. But the men trying to help Sara seemed to know what they were doing. Just like they were skilled on the battlefield, they clearly skilled in the art of medicine work. Once he was finished placing Mindu back in his wheelchair, Marik handed one of the men a pair of pliers. That way, this man could pull the bullet out of Sara's side.

"What's that!?" Sara squealed, her face turning bright red.

"We need to get the bullet out," one of Vensyr's men

insisted. He placed the pliers into Sara's side, ripping the bullet out of her. He motioned for me to approach.

"What is it?" I asked him.

"She needs someone she cares for, someone she's close to," he told me, pulling a long, surgical needle from a pouch beneath his cloak. "Hold her hand; do anything to distract her."

Sara saw the needle; she squealed. That's when I put one finger to my lips and made a shushing sound. *"It's okay,"* I whispered. *"It's going to make it better...."*

"Bu—"

"Sara—"

"I don't want to die!" she screamed.

"You're not going to die!" I told her. "They just need to sew up your wound."

The knight holding the needle hesitated.

"Do it," I told him. "The sooner it's done, the sooner she'll be in her right mind again."

The needle was in! Sara squealed again, grabbing my hand so tight that it hurt. But the pain was worth it, because it distracted her from her *own* pain. Only two more stitches and the wound would be closed. One stitch left... *then,* done.

Sara drew in a deep breath, still in pain but otherwise all right. I lifted her body and approached Marik. "She needs rest," I said.

"Oh *Baby-boy*, ain't that the truth," Marik replied. "Follow me. I'll get the princess a bed to sleep on in a *jiffy!* She can rest below deck while the ship makes its way for Alexandretta."

I smiled. "Thank you."

Marik winked and smiled back. "No problem, *Sweet-cheeks!*"

***

As a violet twilight overcame the horizon, I watched as the fortress city of Alexandretta came into view. It was a large city, capable of holding at least ten thousand members of the resistance. Its gates were as black as oil, and its tallest buildings were white like snow. The city was protected by Sky Flails, just like the ones that protected the Imperial City. Yes, Tiberius had his throne. And yes, the resistance had lost its base at Alma Defa. But Sara would reign as ruler in the fortress stronghold of Alexandretta.

Sara was soon able to walk on her own. Yes, Gibbs's bullet had weakened her. And his betrayal *did* seem to rip her self-confidence and her judge of character to shreds. But I made sure to tell her that it could've been far worse. At least she was still alive, which was better than I could say for Gibbs. If anything, Gibbs's betrayal of her had made her realize that it was time to begin planning an end to the war. Once we were inside Alexandretta, I knew she would get things moving so we could do just that.

And we were closer to that moment than ever before. Soon, *The White Gauntlet* had docked inside the city's docking bay, and the ship's doors opened to allow several leaders of the resistance onboard. This included a man with a scarlet eyepatch and fiery-red hair, plus Hugo and Rookwood as well. They were among some of the highest-ranking soldiers I'd ever met, each wearing armor of higher quality than I could ever hope to afford. Hugo was walking toward me, of course, but he wasn't the only one. In fact, all of them were approaching me and Sara.

Hugo threw his arms around me. "Thank the gods you're safe. I figured the attack on Alma Defa wouldn't be good."

"Thank you for your concerns, Lord Salcroth," Sara said.

Hugo loosened his embrace over me, looking at Sara. "As a father, I'd be crazy not to be worried. Alex is my child too, after all."

"Where's Vensyr?" Rookwood asked, removing his triangle hat. He seemed surprised that the man was missing. "And Gibbs?" he added.

"Gibbs betrayed us," I told Rookwood, "and Tiberius shot Vensyr in the head."

"No…" he said, clutching his chest.

"That's not good at all," said the man with a scarlet eyepatch.

"We'll avenge him," I said, revealing Excelsior under my cloak. "Gibbs is already dead, so are two of Tiberius's generals. I'd say that if we want to end this war within the next few weeks, we're already close to making that happen."

"I agree," Hugo said. "But we've still got some work to do before we can attack the Imperial City."

"Like what?" Sara asked.

"We've just received word that Tiberius is having his knights attack resistance-friendly towns again.[79] I've received orders to lead two hundred knights to look for survivors. Once this is done, I will bring what knights I can here. Then together, we will head to the Imperial City for the final battle."

"When do you leave?" I asked.

"In two hours."

Given the situation, I couldn't blame Hugo for leaving. But that's not to say I wouldn't miss him. "Okay," I said, "but it's good to see you again."

"Likewise," Hugo replied. "Now, if you'll excuse me, I should go find Alex and say goodbye before I can't."

When Hugo was gone, the man with the scarlet eyepatch stepped forward. "Mr. Bellbrook, I am Isaac Lewis," he said, bowing his head; Rookwood and the other men did as well. "I am the Governor of Alexandretta."

"He's the reason I escaped Tiberius when he took

---

79 Part of the Purge of Resistance.

over Isobellia," Sara said. "He pretty much raised me,"[80] she added.

"I've made sleeping arrangements for you at *The Blue Phoenix Inn,*"[81] Lewis continued. "It's all bought and paid for, straight out of my personal savings. If there's anything else you need, let me know."

"Thanks, Isaac," Sara told the man, leaning forward to kiss his cheek. "You did always spoil me."

"Anything for you, Highness," Lewis replied, pointing his head toward the airship's door. "You may go ahead into the city if you like, or you can go to the inn for rest. Either way is fine."

---

80 On the eve of his death, Michael Willington placed his daughter Sara in the care of Isaac Lewis (one of his Royal Guards), and sent them into hiding. For many years, Isaac and Sara lived life on the run from the Empire. It wasn't until her sixteenth birthday that Sara decided she was tired of running and chose to begin a revolution.
81 The refugees from Alma Defa were also given shelter, but in *The Brown Fox Inn* of the Housing District rather than *The Blue Phoenix Inn* of the Industrial District.

14

As I woke one morning in mid-August, the princess was laying beside me. For a few minutes, we laid under the sheets, looking at each other. Then after kissing me on the cheek, Sara said, "That was the best night's sleep I've had in weeks."

At half past eight, there was a knock at my door. So, I slipped on a robe and answered it at once. It was Alex and Rookwood. I could tell by looking at Alex that she was upset. Her eyes were drenched in tears, after all.

"Alex, what's wrong?" I asked; Alex didn't answer.

Sara came up beside me, wearing a robe like mine.

"Highness…" Rookwood said at once. "What are you doing here?"

"I've been having nightmares since Gibbs shot me," Sara told him. "Being close to someone at night has been helping me sleep."

"Well, in any case, I need you to meet us at the tavern

in the Business District," Rookwood said. "There's a recent development that we need to discuss. And André?"

"Yes?" I replied.

"Prepare for the worst."

That's when I closed the door and began to get dressed.

***

As quickly as possible, Sara and I dressed ourselves and made our way for the Inner-City Train Station.[82] Soon, we boarded a bullet train[83] bound for Alexandretta's Business District. Less than an hour after waking, I had gone from being perfectly fine to being very anxious. I didn't know what would be revealed once we reached the tavern. All I knew was it couldn't be good.

I could tell Alex was upset by what was going on, and let's face facts: Alex rarely got upset. But whatever had happened had done the trick. This made me wonder if it was about something closer to home than just the war. Had Hugo been hurt? *Killed,* even? I didn't want to consider this possibility, but if it was true, then Alex certainly had reason to be upset.

Sara and I reached the tavern, entering while holding hands. As we passed through the bar, Sara and I spotted Rookwood, sitting at a long table with Governor Lewis and

---

82 A train station that connects every major district of Alexandretta.

83 A type of train (invented by Beavis T. Jones) capable of traveling 250 miles per hour, sped up by steam and natural magic.

several other men. Elves and wizards were also present; this included Rubin Mindu. I could also see Alex at the end of the table (still as devastated as ever), and sitting next to her was a man I'd never met before. Sara didn't seem to know him either, but Rookwood did. I got the sense that he'd known this man as long as Vensyr, if not longer.

This man might have been the informant of this recent development, but I wasn't sure. Everyone except Mindu stood to greet me and Sara. Then as we sat, they sat, and I looked at Rookwood on the opposite side of the table. "So, what's going on?" I asked him.

"Well, André…" Rookwood began, but he soon fell silent. I didn't know what this meant. All I *did* know was what I'd been told. "I can't tell him, Cody," he said after a moment. "It's too close to home. Hugo's my friend, after all."

"Then permit me to speak, Aldric," came a very hoarse voice. All eyes were on the man sitting next to Alex, just as the man in question leaned forward. "My name is Cody Wolfsbane," he said, running his many-ringed fingers through his jet-black hair. "I am the leader of a team of resistance knights."

"Nice to meet you," I said.

"My men and I were on a mission to liberate a few resistance-friendly towns, and we succeeded. Heck, even my sister Elsa managed to kill General Darius. However, we traced the Imperial Knights' movements south and found them attacking Windull. Unfortunately, there was no hope. The city was taken, but in the alleyways, I met someone I believe you know."

"Hugo?" I asked.

"Yes," Wolfsbane replied. "My men gunned down several Imperial Knights, but General Morfang used this to his benefit. He grabbed Lord Salcroth; then, he told us that if we want him alive, the Kingslayer must surrender himself, returning Excelsior to the Black King. He's giving you a week. Whether you have an army or not, you must meet Tiberius in his throne room."

As I spoke with General Wolfsbane, I began to realize something. This war was no longer about politics. Not for me, anyway. With Hugo in Imperial custody, things had just become far more personal than ever before. Tiberius was no longer interested in playing games, and all his other moves *were* games compared to this one. He could kill Hugo at any moment, after all. This wasn't the Emperor's first attempt to draw me out into the open, but it *was* the first time it had worked.

I looked at Wolfsbane. "Tiberius is hitting me where it hurts most."

"That's an understatement," he replied. "What makes things worse is that Tiberius is close to locating the last Relic of Redisy: the one he's been after for the last three decades."[84]

---

84 The Everlasting Flame. If Tiberius had succeeded in obtaining this

"He is?" Mindu said from across the table.

"Yes," Wolfsbane replied. "What do you suggest we do?" he asked, looking at me.

"I'm going to have to face Tiberius one day," I said. "Might as well take the bait."

"Sir—"

"Now is not the time to argue, Wolfsbane," I interrupted. "Hugo is the closest thing I've ever had to a father. Like I said, I'm going to have to face him one day. *I* have Excelsior; Lyra's prophecy was about *me*. It makes no difference that Tiberius is close to locating the last Relic of Redisy. He's already very powerful as it is. He's pushed the resistance to the brink, where Alexandretta is our only safe haven. Yes, it's an all right place to live, but it's one of Isobellia's only free cities. I cannot have that, especially after seeing what the Empire is capable of."

"The devils are in our ranks," Sara said, pulling her hand away from mine and running it through her hair. "Gibbs, for example. I thought I could trust him, but he shot me and could've killed me. You need to understand that we have a limited amount of time. Gibbs betrayed me, and

---

Relic, it would've meant certain doom for Sara Willington's resistance. It is the most powerful Relic of Redisy, granting the person who wields it the ability to create legions of angels to do their bidding. With the Everlasting Flame (and the other Relics of Redisy at his disposal), Tiberius would have succeeded in his quest for world domination.

sooner or later, Tiberius could have someone betray André. Then all hope will be lost."

"A few months ago, General Gertrude killed a boy named Luke, who was like a brother to me. That's why I'm in this war. Looking at him, seeing the bullets in his chest…. That's what made me want to destroy the Empire. And my godfather isn't *just* my godfather. He's also the man who raised me. So, let's end this debate and discuss what we're going to do about saving him."

I looked at Alex. From what I could tell, Sara and I had described *exactly* what she was feeling.

"My apologies," Wolfsbane conceded. "I just don't want to see you get killed."

"I don't plan on it," I told him.

Sara looked at Rookwood and said, "Can you contact Marik Katsa and his wife? We need their aid."

"You plan on an aerial attack?" I asked.

"Air, ground, sea…. I want to hit the Imperial City from all fronts. This is crucial, because we cannot have Tiberius escape. We have to corner him; then, *you* will kill him once this is done."

"Even when you put it like that, Highness, the Imperial City will be hard to take," Wolfsbane said. "There are Dragonshade Wurms and Sky Flails guarding the city walls—"

"The princess is aware," Mindu said. "We had to get

into the city to steal Excelsior, so naturally we've seen them. The Wizards of the Fifth Order who survived the attack on Drake's Keep are willing to help. They will lead the lesser Orders of Wizards in the fight and grant the knights on the ground safe passage into the city. We haven't decided on how we're going to do that yet, but we'll figure it out. We always do."

"You talk as if you'll be fighting with us," I said.

"That would indeed be foolish," Mindu replied. "But I *will* help plan the attack with my fellow mages."

The meeting was over. So, with nothing left to say, Sara and I rose from our seats, making it clear that the time of battle was at hand. Alex then stood as well, and together, we walked out the tavern door.

15

As I STOOD at the edge of *The White Gauntlet,* Sara came
to meet me. The fleet of airships approached the Imperial
City; the battle was at hand.[85] The moment I'd been waiting
on was finally here. I could tell by the look in her eyes that
Sara was terrified of the moments to come. Not that I could
blame her. I was frightened too. Any wrong move could get
me killed. Or Hugo, for that matter. If Tiberius could kill

---

85 The Imperial Siege—also known as the Battle of Lyonisis—was a massive campaign directed at the Imperial City. The resistance's goal was to
surround the city from every theater of war. That way, there was little
chance that the Black King Tiberius could escape with his life.

In the air was a fleet of 500 ships (led by *The White Gauntlet*), most of
them from either Issylot or Alexandretta.

On the ground were hundreds of resistance fighters (led by Aldric
Rookwood and Cody Wolfsbane). Excluding the knights of General
Wolfsbane, most of the ground troops were either from Alexandretta or
one of the cities destroyed in the Purge of Resistance.

The elves of Alma Defa also took part. Their ex-governor (Gilthoyd
Elfynstone) led a small fleet of warships to provide the resistance with
some much-needed backup.

Vensyr (his own flesh and blood), I knew he could kill Hugo just for the heck of it. At that moment, he was probably preparing to do just that, or worse. All I knew for sure was that Excelsior was my only hope of saving my godfather.

Sara took my hand as Alex came up behind us. Together, the three of us looked off in the distance. I saw the Imperial City coming into view. Just as before, Sky Flails and Dragonshade Wurms protected the city. Behind it, storm clouds were gathering: so dark that the skin of the Wurms nearly blended in with them. Thunder boomed like a kettle drum, and Sara took this as a cue to get things moving.

She motioned Marik in our direction. "Yes, Your Majesty?" he said.

"Move *The White Gauntlet* in attack position," she told him, looking at the airships that would follow. "Use your Bynch Book and tell the ships to fire upon the Sky Flails and the Wurms. Also, signal to the wizards. Tell them to ready their spells."

"I'll have it done in a *jiffy!*"

A few minutes later, the fleet flew over the Wurms and the Flails, dodging them but at the same time dropping bombs to destroy them. Unfortunately, these obstacles would not be easily destroyed, but luckily we had a backup plan. There were Wizards of every Order on the ground below,[86] using their combined skills to create Earth Golems

------

86 Two hundred of them or so, led by James Baltimore and other Wizards

to do their bidding. These were massive beasts, each armed with a sword of iron. With these blades, the Earth Golems moved toward the Imperial City, granting safe passage to the knights on the ground. Many Golems sliced the heads off the Dragonshade Wurms and tore apart the Sky Flails that threatened the airship fleet.

Soon, cannonballs fired from the elfish ships of the sea, hitting several Wurms in the head. One of them crashed into the city's largest gate, tearing it away. As I saw this, many knights on the ground charged into the city and clashed with the enemy soldiers that awaited them there.

"What should we do now?" Alex asked.

"The city is breached, so the enemy's distracted," I said, pulling Hugo's magic ring out of the pocket of my battle garments. "Now's our chance." Just then, Sara and Alex grabbed onto me while I slipped the ring onto my middle finger. Together, we teleported from the deck of *The White Gauntlet*; then, we landed in the cobblestone streets below.

Hundreds of resistance knights followed our lead, using broomsticks and other magical means to move into the

---

of the Fifth Order. Their goal was to use their combined spells to make sure the ground troops led by Wolfsbane and Rookwood made it into the city alive.

To do this, they created an army of Earth Golems. The First, Second, and Third Orders used their spells to create their bodies; the Fourth Order conjured their swords of iron; and the Fifth Order used their best animation spells to bring the creatures to life.

streets below. Alex, Sara, and I passed through an alleyway, hitting some of the same roads we'd traveled down the night of Vensyr's death. Soon, we reached the Royal District, entering another alleyway. That's when I saw the palace off in the distance.

"Hey look!" Alex said, pointing down the alleyway in the castle's direction. "The palace isn't far."

I gave her a nod. "Let's go," I told Alex and Sara. "You heard what Wolfsbane said. Tiberius wants me to meet him in the throne room. Let's not disappoint."

Together, we ran down the alleyway, dodging the bullets that came our way. My heart was racing; very soon, it would all be over. With every inch closer that I came to the palace, the closer I'd come to facing my enemy.

I was ready for him; ready to end this once and for all.

We reached the palace doors, and—after killing the men on guard—we entered the palace stronghold and ran up the nearest stairwell. As we reached the throne room, Tiberius was sitting on his throne. Magnus stood next to him, and Ravana wasn't far, aiming her wand at Hugo's head.

"Hello, Tiberius," I said.

Tiberius stood, approaching Hugo as Magnus followed. "It's about time," he said coldly, pulling his flintlock from his cloak. "I must say, I have *so* been looking forward to this. Now, I can show the resistance who's *really* in control!"

"And how convenient! He brought the princess too!"

Ravana said, looking at Magnus and pointing at Sara with one finger. "Saves us the trouble of hunting her down!"

"She's the leader of the resistance," I said, pointing Excelsior right at Tiberius. Sara activated her flintlock's bayonet. "Of course I'm going to bring her along. Now, release my godfather."

"Make me," Tiberius replied.

"I've come," I said. "Isn't that what you wanted? What's the point in keeping a hostage when your demands have already been met?"

"The point?" Tiberius sneered. "The *point*, Bellbrook, is that I want to send a message to those who wish to rebel against me. I want them to know that if they cross me," he added, looking at Hugo, "I will not hesitate in killing their loved ones. I'm going to start with yours."

"*What!?*" I said at once. "Why?"

"Because the people must see who their king *really* is."

"You're no king. You're a murderer," Alex said. "If only the people could've—"

"*Hold your tongue!*" Tiberius bellowed; then, the room fell silent. He returned his attention toward me, pointing his flintlock right at Hugo's head. "And Bellbrook, stay where you *freakin'* are, or I'll kill your godfather in the same fashion I did your parents. I highly doubt you want a point-blank bullet in his *freakin'* little head!"

"You *monster!*" Hugo said, looking Tiberius right in the eye.

Tiberius kicked him in the face, knocking him to the floor. He then holstered his gun and slid a dagger from his cloak, flashing the magical ring on his middle finger. "Better to be an *immortal* monster than a senile old fool like you! In any case, I'm done talking. The only sounds I want you to make are your cries of horror as you watch me slay your godson!" Tiberius turned to Magnus and Ravana. "Kill the others," he told them. "Bellbrook is mine."

Magnus and Ravana ran past me to distract my only aid. Magnus fought Alex and Sara took on Ravana in the closest duels I'd ever seen my allies fight. I'd be lying if I said I didn't want to aid them, but Tiberius was too much of a threat. That's why I focused on the Black King, ready to face him at last.

A moment later, we had engaged each other, only inches away from Hugo. With every move I made, I did my best to protect him. And with every strike I threw, I tried to eliminate my enemy once and for all. But even with Excelsior at my disposal, this duel wouldn't be easy. After all, Tiberius was the finest duelist I'd ever faced.

Suddenly, I felt a punch to the balls; then, my body sank to the marble floor of the throne room. The world as I knew it was about to end. Tiberius was near, raising his dagger over me. Within a moment, the Kingslayer would be dead.

Or so I thought.

Right then, Sara knocked Ravana to the floor, lurching in front of Tiberius as she pointed her flintlock's bayonet at him. "I will not allow you to hurt him!" she demanded.

I didn't have much time. Another moment, and Tiberius would try to kill her. At once, I grabbed Excelsior and stood to face my enemy. But before I could intervene, Tiberius had disarmed Sara, raising his dagger to her throat. That same moment, Magnus pointed his pistol at Alex; then, Ravana raised her wand, aiming it at Hugo.

My entire situation had just changed. Sara, Alex, and Hugo were now at risk of dying. To make matters worse, I had little chance of saving all three.

"Sara…" I said. "Alex…."

"Don't make another sound," Tiberius demanded.

"André!" Sara squealed.

"Do not speak again, or you're dead!" Tiberius said.

I looked from Sara, to Alex, to Hugo. I didn't know what Tiberius was about to do, though it wasn't hard to figure out. His cruelty had grown predictable. Nothing he did or said surprised me anymore.

"Now," Tiberius declared, "you will pay for your crimes, Bellbrook. But I *will* show you a tad bit of mercy. I will allow you to save one of your friends, but *only* one. *Who will it be!?* Your godfather? His daughter? Or the princess, Sara Willington? Better decide quick, or all three will bite the dust!"

I had never felt so conflicted. If I chose to save one of them, I'd be condemning the other two to die mere seconds later. It was an impossible decision: one that I couldn't bring myself to make. All I could do was watch helplessly as the war claimed three more innocent lives.

But soon something happened that I didn't expect. Hugo hadn't spoken since calling Tiberius a monster, but now he cleared his throat to speak again. "André," he said to me. "Before I die, I want to tell you something. Sara is the rightful heir to the Imperial Throne, and Alex is my beautiful daughter. In life, it is a man's responsibility to protect his family, even if it results in his death. If I haven't taught you anything else as your godfather, I hope that you remember that. Just do me one last favor. Protect. The. *Princess!*" Immediately, he snapped the wand from Ravana's grip, firing a spell and blasting Magnus into the backrest of Tiberius's throne.[87]

I charged Tiberius, knocking the dagger away from Sara's throat. The entire room was in an uproar as Magnus scrambled to his feet and Sara pulled her flintlock off the floor, but this was just the distraction Tiberius needed. While no one else was looking, he pulled a white wand from

---

87 *Strikklys:* A basic spell that knocks over its target.

his cloak and aimed it at Hugo. It was one of the Relics of Redisy.[88] "Andreas Bellbrook isn't the only one who controls a Relic of Redisy, and soon I will possess them all! This is the Wand of Power, Salcroth, and it is the deathstick[89] of your demise!"

Tiberius shot his wand at Hugo, unleashing a jet of blue fire upon him. It was easily the most powerful spell I'd ever seen. At once, it sent Hugo's body flying into the air, turning him to ash as he hit the throne room's granite walls.[90]

I couldn't believe what just happened. Hugo—my godfather and the man who raised me—had just been viciously murdered. I clenched my fist around the hilt of Excelsior, looking into the Emperor's single eye. His lack of remorse and callused demeanor was enough to chill me to the bone. Alex might have been crying over Hugo's untimely death, but Tiberius seemed quite pleased with himself.

"Don't look at me like that," Tiberius said, aiming his wand now at me. "He defied me. All I did was enact justice!"

I rolled my eyes. "I have seen *your* justice. You don't even know the meaning of the word! You're vile and cruel, and I think it's time for you to die, *Jenison!*"

---

88 The Wand of Power. This Relic is the most powerful wand in existence. It is so powerful, in fact, that most Wizards of the Fifth Order cannot defeat the duelist who wields it under normal circumstances.
89 A wand used in killing a person or a creature.
90 *Incintricus:* A fire spell designed to burn its target. Coupled with the Wand of Power, this sorcery is capable of killing its target instead, turning them to ash.

"Magnus, Ravana!"

Magnus and Ravana both faced their king. "Yes, my lord?" Magnus replied.

"Kill the others," he said for the second time. "This is where I kill Bellbrook once and for all."

Sara and Alex were ready for them. "Kill him, André," Alex told me, motioning toward Tiberius. "Do it for Dad. *And* Luke."

I nodded, aiming Excelsior at Tiberius. "It's time to finish this," I told him.

"Let's duel!" Tiberius agreed, still pointing his wand at me.

I charged Tiberius, knowing full well that the fate of an Empire depended on the outcome. But this fight was no longer about freeing my people. It hadn't been since Hugo's capture. *But now that Hugo was dead?* I wanted revenge, to kill His Majesty for the death of my fallen godfather. It was thinking about this terrible injustice that had me hitting at Tiberius with my most powerful blows. But Tiberius was skilled with a wand. He was able to block me every time I tried to hit him.

"Die, you *bastard!*" he yelled, throwing a black whip of thorns from the wand,[91] wrapping it around Excelsior.

For a moment, we were locked in battle: me with

---

91 *Battlethorne:* A combat sorcery, designed to turn a wand into a close-range weapon.

Excelsior, Tiberius with the whip of thorns from his own Relic. I glanced momentarily at Alex, taking her pistol and shooting Magnus in the head. Tiberius was so shocked by this turn of events that he wasn't paying attention to me anymore. And with that, our duel was over. I yanked on his whip of thorns, simultaneously disarming the Black King. Victory, it seemed, was in my grasp. But at that moment, Ravana leapt between us and knocked me to the floor.

"What's the deal?" Sara yelled at Ravana, resetting her flintlock's bayonet and reloading its four barrels.

"I'll kill *you* in a moment!" Ravana yelled back.

I charged at Ravana. She fought with her wand, and I with the blade of Excelsior. At once, the magic within Excelsior grew more powerful, as if the blade was a part of my own body. Every move Ravana made was futile, because Excelsior gave me the skills of a master swordsman. It was as if I was no longer fighting, and a much better swordsman—like St. Aramara—was dueling her in my stead. Not even her most powerful spells could harm me, because Excelsior allowed me to block each one with incredible ease.

I blocked one last spell (a ball of red fire);[92] then, I sliced Ravana's wand in half, pushing her to the floor. She was defenseless now, with no weapon to protect herself.

---

92 *Deathfyre:* A spell capable of killing anyone who touches its searing hot flame. While very powerful, this sorcery is easily learned by non-wizards, but only by those who've carefully studied how to use it.

"You're not killing me!" Ravana said defiantly, reaching for her master's wand.

I swung my sword, slicing her left arm clean off her body. Ravana wailed in pain, clutching her wounded limb. After a second or two, however, she took a flintlock pistol out of her cloak and aimed it at my head. "Die, *Kingslayer!*" Ravana yelled, but I moved too quickly for her to fire. Within seconds, I grabbed the pistol with my spare hand, cutting her throat with the blade of Excelsior.

"Ravana!" Tiberius screamed, watching as his last, loyal general fell to the shiny floor of the throne room.

"She's dead," I said, kicking my enemy's weapons away from him. "And you're about to join her."

"That's treason!" Tiberius said as I approached, pulling the man's flintlock out of its holster and tossing it onto the pile of his other weapons. "*I* am the Black King—"

"And one day, we'll have a new White King! Black King, *White* King.... It makes no difference! I guess it never occurred to you that you actually have to be good to your people to gain their allegiance." I grabbed Tiberius by the throat, placing my blade next to it. "I guess you're just too *stupid* to figure that out!"

"How dare you?"

I didn't answer his question. Instead, I asked one of my own. "Tell me," I said, "why should I permit you to live?"

"I have the right—"

"That's *bullcrap!*" Alex interrupted, looking up at her father's ashes. "My father and brother are *dead* because of you!"

"You're pathetic," I told Tiberius. "You've killed thousands, maybe more. You *murdered* my mother and father. You killed King Michael Willington and his wife. You even had the nerve to kill my godfather, yet still, you feel no remorse?"

Tiberius said nothing.

"Speechless, I see," I continued. "As should be expected. You are, after all, just a pathetic little worm."

"*Lies!*" Tiberius screamed.

I kicked Tiberius right in the face.

The Black King choked on his own blood. "*Who the devil do you think you are!?*" he yelled, reaching for the wand that killed Hugo.

I stomped on it; then, pulling Tiberius up, I pushed Excelsior back to his throat. "You can call me whatever you want. Enemy, *bastard....*" I paused. "You know what I'm about to do," I continued. "So as far as I'm concerned, you can call me your executioner. It's who I am, after all. That's the job I was assigned to do. It wasn't *my* choice; rather, it was my destiny."

My speech was finished. So, I held my sword high and slashed Tiberius through the throat. The man's lifeless head then came toppling down from his body, landing on the ground with a loud *thud*. A significant rush of relief over-came me that moment. I was no longer a fugitive. My task was done, my journey ended. Next thing I knew, Sara flung her arms around me and kissed me on the lips. Every trial, every tribulation that I'd been through had put me where I was now. I was more than just a hero. I was Isobellia's savior.

Alex approached, drying out her eyes.

"Let's go outside," Sara said, releasing me from her embrace. "Our victory must be declared."

"Okay," I said.

Together, Sara, Alex, and I walked out of the Imperial Throne Room. I knew that Hugo's death would hurt for many weeks, or many months to come. But I had to be strong, because my people needed me.

Now, more than ever.

EPILOGUE

July 1st, 1442

IT WAS HER birthday. It was the first day of July, and it was as beautiful as Isobellia had become in the fifteen years following the Great Revolution. Today, I took Lucy—my oldest child—out shopping while her mother[93] prepared the palace for a feast of celebration. Not far from us was Alex's husband Cody. He was watching over us in a nearby alleyway, for fear that an onlooker might try to spill Royal Blood.

The Imperial City was bustling with life. Throughout the Royal District, there was a marketplace with different kinds of booths, selling merchandise of all shapes and sizes.

---

93 Andreas Bellbrook married Queen Sara Willington in September of 1427, less than a month after the war had ended.

Jugglers and gypsies crowded the streets of the Royal District as Lucy and I reached a booth on the farthest corner.

"Daddy, look at that!" Lucy said, clutching my hand so we wouldn't get separated. She was a beautiful girl of fourteen, and was the spitting image of her mother. The only difference between the two was that Lucy had jet-black hair, and she had inherited my sapphire eyes. "Daddy?" she repeated.

I turned to see what she had responded to. That's when I saw Wizards of the First Order, conjuring spells from their own booth with wands they had for sale. One of them had shot a simple animation spell from his wand, making a pair of old boots tap-dance without aid.[94] "You like magic a lot. Don't you, Lucy?"

"Sure do," Lucy said, smiling up at me with the same dimpled grin that belonged to her mother. "Magic fascinates me. Wish I could do stuff like that with a wand."

"You can learn," I said.

"I know."

"All you really need is practice," I added, motioning my head toward the booth with the wizards. "I can tell just by looking that they're new. Maybe the First Order. Before I became king, I met a Wizard of the *Fifth* Order."

------

94 *Animatus:* The most basic kind of animation spell. It's far more powerful cousin (*Animophus*) was used during the Imperial Siege by the Wizards of the Fifth Order to create its army of Earth Golems.

"You did?" Lucy said, interested immediately.

"Indeed," I replied. "Before he died, I saw his magic at work. Those wizards' spells are nothing compared to his. Trust me, Lucy, if you want to learn skills like the ones my friend had, you'll be more than able to. You can do anything if you set your mind to it."

"Who was he?" Lucy asked, stepping toward the wizards' booth and looking at some ivory wands in the display case. "Your friend, I mean," she added.

"Rubin Mindu," I said. Lucy's eyes appeared glued to the ivory wands on display, yet I could tell she was still listening to what I had to say. "After the Great Revolution, he was on my short list of people to become a lord on the Royal Council. Your godmother spent a fair deal of time with him too," I added, "helping him get around in his wheelchair."

"Alex knew him too?"

"Yeah," I replied, pulling a gold shilling from the pouch beneath my cloak and passing it to one of the wizards behind the booth. "I'll take an ivory wand," I told him. The wizard handed me an ivory wand with a scarlet handle, and I passed it into Lucy's small hands. "Happy birthday," I said, looking at my pocket watch. It was one o'clock. "Well, we'd better be off to the castle," I told Lucy, motioning Cody out of his hiding place. When he began to approach, I added, "Your mother will be wondering where we are."

"Okay," Lucy said with a smile, just looking at her birthday present.

As I looked down the market square, I thought of all the blessings the gods had granted me. Despite how much losing my parents, Hugo, and Luke still pained me, the loved ones I'd lost in the past had been replaced by many new ones.

That alone made me happy.